When Mothers and Fathers Work

Creative Strategies for Balancing Career and Family

Renee Y. Magid

with
Nancy E. Fleming

amacom

American Management Association

Library of Congress Cataloging-in-Publication Data

Magid, Renee Yablans, 1934–
    When mothers and fathers work

    Bibliography: p.
    Includes index.
    1. Dual-career families—United States. 2. Married
people—Employment—United States. I. Fleming, Nancy
II. Title.
HQ536.M275   1987   306.8′7   86-47817
ISBN 0-8144-5671-5

Printing number

10 9 8 7 6 5 4 3 2 1

For
David
For the gift of
sharing, caring, and loving

Preface

The decision to write this book was the result of a variety of experiences, both personal and professional. Requests in the last five years for information, technical assistance, and research in the area of employer initiatives in child care have been overwhelming. And yet, even as I was deeply immersed in fulfilling these requests, I somehow knew that the focus for my activities was too narrow in scope, that in looking exclusively at employer-sponsored child care I was only catching a glimpse of a larger picture. The whole picture came into focus when I recognized that the larger and more significant issue in contemporary society was the balance of work and family—not solely employer involvement in child care. I felt it was necessary to have working parents tell their story—the work/family story. I wanted to know how working parents perceived their needs, the major roadblocks in their lives to integrating a career and a personal life, and—most important—what solutions working parents devised that allowed them to succeed with their work/family journey. Thus the seeds for this book were sown.

I decided early on not to include a critical analysis of whether parents should work, and instead accept the current social patterns. Working parents—men *and* women—are here to stay! Decisions to work and parent are personal ones based on a special mix of important factors for each family, as was evidenced by the working parents interviewed. Therefore, this book is intended to encourage, not discourage, working parents. For too long working parents have had to lament what *others* think and fear their disapproval. For too long working parents have been led to believe that wanting both to work and to parent implies neglect of one's children, irresponsibility, selfishness—even, as one grandparent said, "insanity." I, however, have remained optimistic about the integration of work and family, because families throughout history have undergone transition, challenge, and change. They have obviously survived. After much research and hundreds of interviews with working parents and employers, there is no reason for me to believe that this Generation with Choices will not survive as well.

I believe that my association with Nancy Fleming has allowed me to bring a broad perspective to the issues presented in this book, because Nancy and I come from different backgrounds—on the surface seemingly worlds apart. One of us is recently married, childless, and part of a dual-career marriage; the other married and a working parent through many years of rearing two children. I feel that this divergence in background has deepened my understanding of a complex topic. Our collaboration, with each other and with the working parents interviewed, has been rewarding.

One caveat is in order concerning the language contained in this book. All parents work, whether they are paid for their labor or not. However, I restrict the phrase "working parents" to include only those parents who are engaged in paid employment.

Renee Yablans Magid

Acknowledgments

First and foremost, I want to express my appreciation to Nancy Fleming for her skill, advice, and perception. Our discussions and debates served to make sense of a complicated issue.

This book owes much to the efforts of many people besides the author. This project could never have come to fruition without the willingness and dedication of all the working parents who allowed me to interview them—who shared their precious time, their joys, their fears, and their hopes for the future. The working parents I interviewed came from every area of the country. However, many working parents responded to my requests for people to participate in the interviews because of the special interest and concern of the Family Resource Coalition in Chicago. Because of this organization's willingness to distribute flyers, send letters, and contact key people in cities around the nation, I was able to interview parents *almost everywhere* in the United States. I could not have done it without the Family Resource Coalition! To everyone who talked with Nancy Fleming and me, a grateful thank-you. To the working parents, thank you for teaching me about the future of American families.

No manuscript gets to the publisher's desk without many hours of editing, typing, and retyping. For this effort, I want to extend my special thanks to Ellen Assman, who cheerfully typed the manuscript with attention to detail and dedication to deadlines and excellence.

I am grateful for the superior efforts of the AMACOM staff who worked to make this book a reality. I appreciate the professionalism, creativity, enthusiasm, and support of Philip Henry, Eva Weiss, Barbara Horowitz, Lydia Lewis, and Consuelo Toledo. My thanks to Janet Frick, who copyedited the manuscript.

Special thanks to Pat Valeno for making time in her hectic work schedule to offer her generous support and help, in order to ensure the success of this project.

I also greatly appreciate the efforts of Jodi Shubin and Anne Throop, who provided not only a sounding board but also a good deal of time checking the details for this book.

Personal Notes

Warmest thanks go to my daughter, Melissa Magid Codkind, who provided superb counsel and gentle support during the planning and writing of the manuscript. She was always there. What more could anyone ask?

To my son, Mitchell Magid, I will always remember his response (at about age seven) to a bad day I was having in trying to merge work and family, when I started taking vows to stay at home all the time. His comment: "But Mommy, what will you do if you don't go to work, *just* stay at home all the time and be *only* a mother?" Perhaps he was way ahead of the times. To Mitchell, thank you for always putting things in perspective for me.

Finally, to my husband, David Magid, loving thanks for *always* believing in me, for supporting my professional activities, for providing honesty coupled with a remarkable brand of humor and keen common sense, and most of all for being his wonderful self!

RYM

Contents

1

For You, the Working Parent

If you are currently a working parent or know you will be one in the future, this book has been written expressly for you. It is about contemporary American parents living and working in a fast-paced and ever-changing technological society; individuals who desperately want to rear their children effectively and experience the joys of parenting, and who also need to pursue paid employment.

Working Parents Today: A Complex Picture

Ten years ago, a book dealing with work and family issues would have been quite different from the one you are now reading. A good deal less concern existed about working parents, for even that recently most families resembled the traditional family picture: the father as sole breadwinner and support of his wife and family, and the mother who maintained the home and was the primary nurturer of the young. That traditional family picture has now altered dramatically. Today you may be a single divorced parent raising a child and working outside the home, or you may be part of a dual-career family team, each involved in very different career goals, but both concerned about family goals. You may even be a man or woman in your mid-thirties, who has been in the workforce since leaving school, has achieved a measure of success in a chosen career, is now experiencing the birth of a first child, and is suddenly faced with linking the worlds of work and family life.

In dealing with the integration of work and family, this book tries not to be naive and overly simplistic about the complex issues and concerns surrounding working parents, and tries not to emphasize the negative reports and research dealing with the effects of working and parenting. Instead, the book acknowledges the following facts, which may make a difference to working parents:

- Parents who work, including parents with young children, are now part of our national way of life.
- More women contribute to family income now than at any other time in the history of the United States, and will continue to do so.
- The concept of the American family now includes a diversity of relationships between people that will have a significant impact on the organizations they work for.
- The attitude of parents toward working and parenting appears more important to the well-being of the family than all other factors.
- More men and women are reevaluating their options for their work lives and personal lives.
- Attitudes and decisions in society tend to lag behind reality.
- Other nations in the Western world are addressing the reality of working and parenting by providing policies that support families where both parents work. The United States is lagging behind reality.

Many books for working parents of young children have dealt with the often conflicting issues of parental employment, the pros and cons of child care, quality versus no-quality child care, child development, and parenting. We have elected to review existing materials, interview working parents and employers throughout the nation, and put together in one book a comprehensive, practical discussion of work and family issues. It is not meant to be read in one sitting, but to serve as a permanent reference book that you can refer to many times. Because we realize that working parents have little of a precious resource known as time, we have included extensive Appendixes to help you efficiently track down additional types of information not included here.

Family Portraits

It is very helpful for working parents to hear from one another about the personal, societal, and cultural roadblocks they have encountered to combining work and family and the unique creative solutions they have developed to manage their lives successfully. As a result, this book offers real family portraits gathered from a cross-section of the nation, through hundreds of personal interviews and written questionnaires, from families who are currently involved in a variety of work settings and family lifestyles. These family portraits offer you a very personal, realistic picture of the obstacles and choices that working parents encounter and the creative strategies that have enabled them to succeed. You will meet the American families we talked with and participate in some of their struggles, their concerns, and their joys. Perhaps you will be able to see your own family more clearly against this composite backdrop of other American families. The portraits are also intended to inspire you, to help you understand that you too have the capacity to balance your work and family lives.

Although this book was never intended to be a ''pure'' scientific study or an attempt at preserving statistical consistency, we were pleased to discover that the working parents we interviewed came from almost every state in the nation, and that in fact there are more similarities than differences among working families throughout the United States.

The Employer's Perspective

Because this book deals with work *and* family, not work *or* family, we felt it was necessary to interview employers as well as working parents. However, we chose not to list the number of companies that have created child-care initiatives, or to concentrate on the myriad of work/family options available to employers. The story of employer-supported child care has already been told elsewhere. (For books on this topic, see Appendix B, Section 6.) We did choose to tell you about the creative solutions for balancing work and family that employers and working parents shared with us, and some of their thoughts on corporate America that may have positive results.

We want to stress that although many people bemoan how few employers in the United States are concerned about work/family issues, changes are being felt by employees and employers that signal new opportunities. Change is a slow process involving values, traditions, and predictable modes of human behavior; to expect to turn the American workplace around all at once is unreasonable.

Unleashing Your Creativity

Your work/family concerns today, or this year, are probably somewhat different from those of yesterday or one year ago. Parenting and working are like a kaleidoscope: constantly shifting yet still containing the same elements. New issues emerge, new solutions are proposed, old issues remain and cry out for confrontation.

This book does not try to tell you what is right and wrong for your family, since your family is different from any others, and special to you. We have attempted to anticipate your questions and dilemmas, not to provide you with prescriptions. We hope that the stories of other working parents, and the problem-solving techniques presented here, will help unleash your creativity so that you can devise your own unique solutions for integrating your work and family lives. Creativity is what replaces working parents' familiar feelings of helplessness and isolation with purposeful, constructive action.

Finally, we hope this book doesn't end for you, or for us, on the last page. If there are creative solutions you want to share with us, obstacles you encounter, issues you continue to have trouble finding help with, or resources suggested in this book that you find particularly helpful, write to the address listed below and let me know. Sharing information and solutions can be a way of keeping step with a rapidly changing society—even, perhaps, of predicting future patterns.

Dr. Renee Y. Magid
Department of Education
Beaver College
Glenside, PA 19038

2

The Generation with Choices

Accustomed as we are to change, or unaccustomed, we think of a change of heart, of clothes, or of life with some uncertainty. We put off the old, put on the new. . . . Every age is an age of transition.

—Josephine Mills,
Poetry and Change

This is a generation of diverse American families, not "the American family"; of breadwinners, not a breadwinner; of work *and* family, not work *or* family. It is, as many parents believe, a transitional generation. Dissatisfied with what we saw as a limited range of options and roles open to our own parents, we strive to become the Generation with Choices. We seek greater choice in the home: who will manage the house, who will nurture and raise our children, where we will live. We seek greater choice in employment: where to work, how to work, when to work.

We aspire to greater choice in our lives because we equate it with freedom. A young couple, both examples of corporate America turned entrepreneurs, explained that the freedom found with greater choice can be used to "decide whatever way we want to do it, to make however much money we want to make, to say when it's time to work and when it's time to take care of our children.''

Freedom to choose is something we want not only for ourselves, but for our children. In the words of parents we spoke with,

- I hope my girls both feel that they have choices in their lives and that they know how to choose the best for themselves and their families. We would like them to say they felt more easily able to choose a lifestyle they liked because they had been acquainted with a variety of possibilities.
- We hope our child will have a lifestyle self-determined by what ''feels right,'' not chosen on the basis of social pressures either way.

Family Portraits

The families described in the following portraits are representative of this transitional generation, the Generation with Choices. (Most of the names used are fictitious, in order to preserve privacy. Where real names are cited, it is with the permission of the people involved.) Perhaps their lives in some way resemble yours or those of your friends and neighbors. Certainly on a day-to-day basis they experience frustrations, conflicts, and anxieties not unlike those of any working parents. In spite of this, these contemporary families have persisted in seeking out and devising creative solutions to work/family issues so that they may continue to be the Generation with Choices.

The sincerity and commitment of the families we met with was quite evident. For example, physicians allowed us to follow them on hospital rounds in order to complete an interview. Some working parents talked to us at 6:00 A.M. or 11:00 P.M. in order to be sure their story was told, and others had lunch with us in fast-food restaurants where we had to search our brains and stomachs afterwards to recall whether we really had lunch. We sent follow-up letters after personal meetings when we wanted to be sure we understood a point or had all the information we needed.

Meet some of the families we talked with! Through their family portraits, we hope you will develop a sense of the full range of work/family patterns open to this generation.

Joan and Mark Miller

The Millers are a dual-career couple whose professional and personal lives are closely interwoven. Both are physicians. They met during college and sustained the arduous years of medical school together. They shared the all-important decisions about the path each would select as a lifetime career commitment. Mark selected public health and Joan selected pediatric endocrinology. Together they decided on having two children. The Millers now have two boys, one 6½ and one 4½. Joan and Mark agree that "it is difficult to have dual careers in one household, especially when those careers are extremely demanding ones—the kind of jobs you can't walk out on at the drop of a hat." As a doctor, Joan explained,

> You don't walk away from a dying child, even if your own child is in a play at school. These are the dilemmas we face each day. The good part is that attending to a dying child versus your own child's needs does not occur too often. In our own way we feel we are helping to improve the quality of life for our patients. While we often feel stressed and sometimes guilty for not being able to do it all, we also feel much pleasure in our lives—both as parents and physicians.

Joan also shared her feelings about motherhood.

> I was always sure that if you handed me a baby—any baby—I could do all sorts of medical things with it. What I wasn't sure of was, did I really have a mother inside of me? We [women] are supposed to be instinctively nurturing and we're not sure if we are. Now that I've had my

own children I know I can do it. It's an incredible experience, parenting! I'm a much better doctor now that I'm a parent. For me mothering is a lot harder than doctoring. The best thing is I know I can be both. Without my job I wouldn't be happy. I'd feel useless. Also, I think my children will be proud of me and I'm a good role model for the other female residents.

Mark noted,

I feel really good that Joan and I are doing exactly what we want to be doing. We have little role definition in our household; we both know what needs to be done, and we do it. I do get upset when I'm not involved with my children.

Mark's need to spend time with his children, he explained, was at least partly behind his decision to enter the public health field.

I often compare our family to other families, and I feel Joan and I share more as a result of the kind of lifestyle we have. The result is that our lives are enriched—all of our lives, including the children's.
Is it all perfect? No, not at all. Nothing ever is. Joan sometimes feels confused and upset, she works too hard trying to keep up with community norms. The way I see it, Joan surpasses the norms. Women have guilt about going to work that men rarely have.

Karen Werner and Gary Conners

We were in our early thirties when our first child was born. This was our situation: We were both working full time and we were both interested in parenting our new baby. Gary did not want to bear the entire burden of being the family breadwinner, and we were committed to spending the early, formative years with our child; we never contemplated full-time day care for her. Given all this we agreed that we would both work only part time (20 to 25 hours a week), and try to arrange our schedules in a complementary way so that one of us would be home with the baby while the other was at work. This meant we would share the financial burden and the parenting role equally.

Our children are now six and four years old. We continued our part-time work, coparenting arrangement, until this fall when financial pressure prevailed and I took a full-time job outside of our home, and Gary continued working 23 hours a week. We have faced many problems making this arrangement work financially, emotionally, logistically, and socially. We have learned a lot from our struggles, both about ourselves and about the role of children, families, and work in our society. For reasons beyond our control it was often difficult, and sometimes it seemed nearly impossible, to continue our arrangements. However, we prevailed and we are proud of our decisions and our accomplishments.

David Robertson

"I'm one of seven in the country," David said jokingly. David is a single father, 100 percent responsible for the care and support of his three-year-old son, Bryan.* David is also a physician involved in cancer research at a world-renowned comprehensive cancer research institution. More than once during the interview, David talked about his good fortune in being able to pursue a career that provides a challenge: "The choice of cancer research, the advances that are ahead—the thrill of doing something really important. I'm doing just what I want to be doing, not what I have to do. There is much satisfaction in that."

David talked a good deal how much he loved his son. During our conversations he often recounted the day Bryan was born.

Suddenly I knew the meaning of life—my whole life snapped into place. I knew that more than anything I wanted to be

---

*Actually, a 1984 census report indicates a total of 271,000 single fathers with children under the age of six who maintain their own homes, and a total of 159,000 single fathers with children under the age of three who maintain their own homes.[1]

> this child's Daddy. My relationship with Bryan has allowed
> me to blossom, to open myself up. It has allowed me to feel,
> to exhibit behaviors I didn't know I was capable of.
> I am the living embodiment of every man's worst fears. I'm
> a prototype of the fear of having to care for your child on
> your own, especially in the formative and generative phase
> of building your career, and also being an individual who
> has a high degree of expectation. Society isn't used to my
> situation—that of a father caring for his child without a
> mother. Mothers are supposed to care for children; they are
> taught to do this. Men, like women, can learn to be nur-
> turing and sensitive to their children.
> Bryan and I have a good life, but it wasn't always that way.
> There were many years of pain as I attempted to deny that
> my wife, my childhood sweetheart, was an alcoholic. I was
> exhausted and overwhelmed at first, until I learned to reach
> out and utilize my support systems. I learned not to expect
> more from myself than I could deliver.

David's employer participates in a child-care consortium,
which operates a child-care center for the children of the parent-
employees from four health-care organizations.

> The worksite center is minutes from my office, and this
> greatly reduces my concerns regarding child care and my
> anxiety about how Bryan is spending his day. The one thing
> I wish I knew earlier was that I could do it and be good at
> it (parenting, that is).

Maria and Tom Starr

Maria, Tom, Grandmom (Tom's mother), James (age 3½), and
Todd (18 months) make up this family portrait. Maria and Tom
are involved in separate but related careers; both are employed
in supervisory positions in social service agencies. They work full
time while Grandmom manages the care of the children and the
house.

Grandmom did not always live with Maria and Tom, but
was asked to come live with them about a year ago. Both Tom

and Maria need to work, for financial and emotional reasons. They felt that Grandmom's presence would not only provide the kind of extended family arrangements that Tom was accustomed to in his childhood, but would enable three generations to learn from one another and be part of a shared experience.

Maria and Tom are comfortable and pleased with their work and family arrangements. Grandmom's comment about the family arrangement was, "My mother took care of my children while I worked and now it's my turn to care for Maria and Tom's children." When we asked Maria and Tom how long they planned to continue their present arrangements, they told us, "Grandmom can stay with us forever, or as long as she is happy."

Beth and Jack Gibbons

Getting up at 4:00 A.M. in order to be at work on time is an everyday occurrence for Beth, the director of a home health-care agency. Jack, her husband, is a controller for a suburban Chicago hospital. Beth drives about 35 miles to work each day, arrives at 5:30 A.M., and leaves about 2:30 P.M. This special schedule, which Beth negotiated with her employer, allows her time to get home to pick up her two children from child care: Jeff, six years, and Jim, two years. It also allows Beth time to go to the library to study for the classes she is attending for her degree in health science, and time for workouts at the gym two days a week. Jack, who works only ten minutes away from home, starts his day about 6:30 or 7:00 A.M. or "whenever the children start their day." The Gibbonses enjoy their work/family arrangement, "for it provides each parent time for individual pursuits, time alone with the children, time for a career, and time with the other."

Edna Hall-Barber and Bob Barber

"Taking turns" is the way Edna and Bob described their dual-career family. For some time, Bob was the primary wage earner, while Edna was the primary caregiver for their twin sons, now 3½ years old. When Bob's company decided to move its headquarters to another state, Edna and Bob chose not to relocate. Earlier Edna and Bob had been examining the advantages and disadvantages of taking turns at parenting and paid employment, and they decided this was the best time to try it. Edna took a job in the field she was trained for, that of a technical writer, and Bob took on the role of primary caregiver and home manager. Edna said, "Most of our friends were betting on how long Bob could last in his new role. We would have made a lot of money if we'd taken them up on it."

"This is the hardest job I've ever had," Bob declared, "mainly because you can't always decide to finish a task later, especially when such things as feeding the kids must be done *now*."

In the near future, Edna and Bob are planning to take turns at being employed part time. One will work while the other takes care of the twins.

Margaret and Calvin Coffey

Margaret and Calvin* view themselves as entrepreneurs. They are both currently self-employed. Margaret conducts her management consulting business from home, while Calvin conducts his rowing shell company from a worksite not far from home. Margaret and Calvin are the parents of three girls, ages seven years, four years, and three months. Before the birth of their second child, Margaret held an executive-level position with a nationally recognized corporation. She left the position about four years ago to go to work as the business manager for the family

---

*Margaret and Calvin Coffey are real names, as is Coffey Corporation. The Coffeys have agreed to have their story told without the use of fictitious names.

business, Coffey Corporation, a position she still maintains along with her consulting business.

Among the reasons for her departure from the national corporation were to be accessible to her children, to cut down on business travel that took her away from home much of the time, and to eliminate the physical and psychological demands associated with her executive-level position.

Margaret recalls the days of her M.B.A. program.

> Professors would respond to my state of motherhood with, "Why are you coming to school when you have a baby?" (This was only a few short years ago). The message that I was getting from the institution was, "You can't be serious." However, I was serious. I graduated and the salary offers were very appealing. I finally decided on a position as a marketing manager for a large growth company. I told them that I would take the position if I could work out satisfactory child-care arrangements. Otherwise, I would accept another offer.
>
> Within six months the organization opened a worksite child-care center with the recognition that if it was going to attract talented women to the organization it needed to address family concerns as well as work-related issues. I loved it all! It wasn't until the birth of my second child that I noted stress-related health problems. While I was well on my way to becoming a vice president, I noticed my freedom was diminishing instead of increasing. I felt I needed to make a decision about my career and my personal life. I decided to resign as marketing manager.
>
> Management responded by calling my resignation a "leave of absence" in the hope I would come to my senses. The corporation was willing to make an exception in my case and extend my six-month leave of absence. However, I felt that unless the organization could think about establishing a policy that would include all women, I didn't want it to make an exception for me. The organization still maintains an office and a secretary for me, for those times I do consulting for it. As a woman with a family

you often need to push for personal options, or you are not likely to get any. I can't deny that having a Harvard M.B.A. has provided me with a passport, a ticket for creating all kinds of options.

I believe that families need to set personal priorities and stick by them. We need to make decisions that do not compromise our happiness and chances for a long life; otherwise it can lead to disillusionment and dissatisfaction in later life.

I haven't dropped out of the workforce, just adjusted my work life to make it work with my family life.

Donna and Michael Mayo

Donna began our conversation by telling us,

> I come from a large family with lots of siblings and relatives. I was used to having lots of people around most of the time. I was unaccustomed to the isolation of a nuclear family arrangement. I've always believed in sharing resources and in spouses not only helping each other but other people as well.

The result was the decision by Donna and Michael to buy an imposing seven-bedroom house in a Midwestern city, which they share with another nuclear family.

Donna (the director of a public advocacy organization), Michael (a communications director), Karen (age 12, from Donna's first marriage), Billy (age 5, adopted) currently live with another family that has a child about the same age as Karen. Together all members of the household share meals, food preparation, shopping costs, cooking, cleaning, and child care. Donna explained,

> What it means for me is I only have to cook about one or two times a week. If I'm going to be late at my office, I can call and ask another adult to get dinner on the stove. It doesn't make sense to have so many isolated people and

nuclear families with so many washing machines, dishwashers, and so on that are unused for much of the time.

We live better because we share resources. We've had virtually no problems with our living arrangements, even though the families sharing our home have not remained constant during the past nine years. We recruit families who share a common value system, and it works, even the unwritten rules about healthy food cooked from scratch.

The people at work, who only see me in my navy blue suit and high heels, are surprised at my family's living arrangements. My coworkers usually refer to it as a commune, sort of a throwback to the 1960s. Actually it's a cooperative sharing arrangement that allows for caring about and for people, for enjoying a variety of people, and for knowing how to share while still maintaining the identity of your family and your own individuality.

Diana Tyler

"Being a single mother is not difficult, *if* you have extended family support systems." This was Diana's comment about her life for the past five years as a single mother with a six-year-old daughter, Heather. Diana feels fortunate that she lives close to her parents, who provide after-school care for Heather and lots of love and nurturing for both Diana and Heather. "I love the way I was parented," said Diana, "and I feel good that my parents are sharing in the parenting of Heather." Monday through Friday evenings, Diana, Heather, and Diana's parents have dinner together, then Diana and Heather return home to their own house to have time together.

In addition, Diana has many brothers and sisters and an active social life as part of her church affiliation. This provides Diana with additional support and friendship. Diana works as the coordinator of a prenatal education program and is able to work out flexible work scheduling as part of her job. She indicated, "I feel very comfortable as a single mother rearing her child. Right now I have little desire to change my life in any way."

Helen and Don Westin

Sharing at home and on the job is the way Helen and Don have arranged their career and family responsibilities. Helen and Don are reporters at a major Northeastern newspaper. They were working at the paper when they planned their family. Before the baby was born, it was agreed that Helen would take the first six months after the baby's birth for maternity leave, followed by Don taking the second six months for paternity leave. This would allow for one year in which at least one parent would be home with the baby.

The arrangements worked so well for both parents, and each felt so satisfied in being able to share parenting, that they decided to attempt to make the arrangement permanent. Helen and Don approached their employer with a plan for job sharing. After much negotiation and what seemed like much time, Helen and Don now share one job and share in the primary caregiving of Cheryl, now two years old.

We asked Helen and Don about the financial repercussions of their decision. Helen responded by telling us that once the decision to live on one salary had been made because of their desire to provide parental care for Cheryl, the job-sharing arrangement emerged as the natural solution. "That way, both of us reap the benefits of being at home and at work. True, we've had to tailor our lifestyle to a more limited budget, but it's been worth it."

Meg and Ron Anderson

"Flexibility has been a big advantage in our family: We take things one step at a time and with luck it all works out well for us." Now after many years of schooling, training, and trade-offs, Meg and Ron feel that they have come up with a workable plan for blending all the factors in their lives. Ron is a medical doctor; Meg is a nurse and a writer.

The Andersons are also the parents of two children, Robin and Steven. Pooling resources, time, money, energy, and child care made it possible for the Andersons to succeed at work and at home.

> We had no long range plan, took it a step at a time, and it happened with luck to work out really well for us. Meg worked while Ron was in medical school, then we switched. Meg was home with kids full time for three and a half years. Robin wanted to go to nursery school (although Meg had planned to stay home till he reached kindergarten). Meg worked part-time at his nursery school to pay its cost and earn some spending money (fifteen hours a week). Steven, age 15 months, went along with them to nursery school. When Steven was 2½, Meg returned to her nursing career full time. Ron, who had just finished his residency and was ready for a change from the high-pressured pace, became full-time house spouse for three years—child care, housework, remodeling our newly purchased house. Meg then wanted to cut her work hours to be with the kids more and have more time to write, so Ron started working part-time and Meg cut back clinic nursing hours. That has continued with minor changes in hours for the past six years. The big advantage has been a lot of flexibility in how we have spent our time, without having to face a big cut in income. . . . A hospice MD (this one anyway) earns about the same per hour as a nurse. We pool all our resources in one account, and agree on how we will spend them. Mutual concern, respect, and understanding have made it possible to work out the logistics of blending all the concerns in our lives and helped us come up with solutions which have worked for us.

Peggy Hart Earle and Bruce Earle

If you were to visit the offices of Hartstrings in Malvern, Pa. (a suburb of Philadelphia), you would immediately be struck by the warmth, conviviality, entrepreneurial excitement, and sense of family that permeate the organization. You would probably be welcomed by Peggy and Bruce Earle,* the founders and princi-

---

*Peggy and Bruce Earle are real names, as is Hartstrings. They have given permission to have their story told without the use of fictitious names.

pals of Hartstrings. The office they share has matching desks that sit back to back, surrounded by hand-made quilts and chintz calico curtains. If the scene sounds too good to be true, it gets better as you get to know Peggy and Bruce and listen to their family portrait unfold.

"Working together" is the phrase Peggy and Bruce repeatedly used to describe the balance of work and family in their household.

Peggy and Bruce work together on the job and at home; and, as Bruce indicated, "The work is easier at Hartstrings than at home." On the job at Hartstrings, Peggy is the president and creative designer, and Bruce is the executive vice president and treasurer, along with the special title assigned by Peggy, that of "Vice President of Mental Health." At home Peggy and Bruce are Mom and Dad to Andy, age five, and Timmy, age three.

Peggy started Hartstrings as a cottage industry to keep busy while Bruce was out of town on business, to encourage her entrepreneurial spirit, and to continue her interest in the field of clothing design—a career she was trained for. Peggy also felt that a "small business at home would be perfect, for she could combine parenting and a career." What Peggy and Bruce did not expect was the rapid and positive response to Peggy's designs. With no experience in sales or marketing, Peggy sold the first season's sample line to Bloomingdale's in New York. That was the beginning of the Hartstrings success story! In 1985 Peggy received the EARNIE award for excellence in designing children's clothes.

During the early growth and development of Hartstrings, Bruce essentially did two jobs, the one he held outside his home and the one he held while helping Peggy achieve her goal. In fact, as Peggy indicated, "I and other married women have a decided advantage in getting a business started because we have the financial and emotional support from our spouses." Bruce took a leave of absence from the company he was working for, one of the "Big Eight" accounting companies, just before Andy was born. Peggy had some complications during her pregnancy and Bruce felt it was crucial to be at home running Hartstrings, which was rapidly growing in size, responsibility, and visibility.

The leave of absence became a permanent one as Peggy and Bruce became partners in Hartstrings.

"We look forward to less time at work, more time at home, and more flexible work schedules. We never want to look back at our family life and have regrets. We don't have any now and we hope it continues."

One of the exciting pieces of the Hartstrings portrait is the child-care center that began with a baby-sitting service for Peggy and Bruce's first child and the child of another employee in the early years of the company. It was extended to all employees and became the Hartstrings Child Care Center. In late 1986 it was expanded again in the new and larger Hartstrings facilities. Now known as the Hartstrings Child Development Center, it is described in more detail in Chapter 6.

Joan Hirsch and Doug Adams

Joan, a 31-year-old law and Ph.D. student, started our conversation with an intense declaration of her feelings about being a wife and mother in 1986:

> I get so irritated when I pick up books and magazines and read about the tremendous problems women and men are having today . . . as though past generations were worry-free and life in the "old days" was ideal. There is no ideal life. I'm convinced of that now, although it's taken me the last ten years to come to that realization. Of course, Doug and I have problems, and some of them seem horrendous at the time we're going through them. I try not to lose sight of the fact, though, that we have a healthy and growing relationship, a great two-year-old daughter, and a lot of confidence in ourselves and each other.

One of the liabilities of her family's lifestyle, Joan acknowledges, is time pressure. She and her husband, Doug, a 30-year-old surgical resident, go for days without more than a half hour or so to relax together and talk. "The time deficit can build up," Doug noted, "without your really being aware of it. All of a sudden, you find yourself realizing you have no idea what the other person's been doing for the past week!''

One of the solutions Doug and Joan found to the time crunch was live-in child care for their daughter, Sara.

> Late at night, especially when Sara was a baby, has always been a time of conflict between our daughter and us. Most of the time, we'd take care of whatever her needs were, but sometimes it was just impossible—like when Sara would be crying and Doug would be at the hospital and I'd be here by myself trying to study. Having a husband who isn't here every third night made me realize how much I need someone else here to help me out.

Joan and Doug declared,

> The bottom line is the fact that we have choices, even though to our parents our arrangements seem insane. We are both able to pursue career goals. Work and family: easy? no; possible? yes; difficult? sometimes; stressful? often; rewarding? absolutely!

Composite: A Diverse Society

The family portraits you have just glimpsed are but a small sample of the hundreds we gathered in the course of writing this book, but even this small sample illustrates the broad diversity of lifestyles and options available to today's working parents. Each contemporary family portrait is unique, but all these parents share a commitment to their careers and to nurturing their children. Each family is meeting the challenge of integrating the work and home with family life in its own creative way. It is a challenge all of us have the capacity to meet, once we allow ourselves to understand our sources of conflict and how to overcome them.

3

American Families: Traditions and Transitions

We can't estimate where we are now, and we certainly can't begin to see where we are going, unless we know where we have been.

—Elizabeth Janeway
Between Myth and Morning

It is not our intent to give you a history lesson in this book, but we do intend to help you view the contemporary American family in its historical context. By witnessing the similarities and differences that have emerged over time, you may feel more comfortable with the direction in which your family is moving, and feel reassured that families have consistently undergone both continuity and change—and come out alive and well!

The Early Settlers' Farms:
A Family Affair

For the first European settlers who came to this country, work and family were a shared experience, an integrated whole, not unlike the experience of some of the families we talked with during our interviews. Large families consisting of mothers, fathers, children, relatives, boarders, and neighbors all joined hands in a struggle to survive. The family farm was the center for work and intimacy. Although there was some division in sex roles—women did most of the housework and men did most of the plowing and log-splitting—both sexes did hard physical work. Everyone pitched in to assure the success of the family farm. Children helped with chores, both in the house and out in the fields, as soon as they were old enough. As families struggled to win food from an often unyielding land, a general spirit of cooperation existed between men and women who worked side by side to earn a living and to care for their children.

Like Margaret and Calvin Coffey, Peggy and Bruce Earle, and Diana and Heather Tyler, families were not separated geographically or socially. The two separate worlds of work and family, so well known to contemporary society were not part of the early American family picture. Children of farm families could enjoy the same kind of opportunities Diana's daughter, Heather, enjoys with her 80-year-old grandfather and 74-year-old grandmother, or the kind of relationship Maria, Tom, Grandmom, James, and Todd Starr have: close association of children with a variety of older adults. Urie Bronfenbrenner, Professor of Human Development and Family Studies at Cornell University, has pointed out that this kind of intergenerational bond "allows human beings to develop to their fullest capacity."[2]

The Industrial Revolution: From Old McDonald's Farm to McDonald's, Inc.

Two related significant phenomena took place in the United States during the late nineteenth century: urbanization and industrialization. Farm families became less typical as more of the country's population became concentrated in the cities. Earning a living was now done away from home by fathers, thus creating a physical separation and division of loyalty unknown earlier to the farm family.

The problems these families faced are not unlike the problems families are facing in the 1980s. The family desperately wanted to continue to function as a basic unit, maintaining family values, but also needed to embrace the new values of a changing society. Mothers and fathers could no longer expect to be involved side by side in paid employment or to share jointly in the care of their children. Parents quickly recognized the changes in child-rearing patterns, in divided loyalty between home and workplace, in less shared time for interpersonal relationships within the family, and in the sharper delineation of the roles of men and women. All these factors still contribute to the recurring tension that plagues many contemporary families. Also, several ideas took root during the industrialization of America that continue to create barriers for working parents today:

- The "doctrine of two spheres," which sharply divides male and female work roles.
- The idea that because children are not adults, they must demand 100 percent of a mother's attention, energy, and resources.
- The belief that the care of young children by people outside the family is okay only in time of crisis.

As men in increasing numbers were employed in jobs away from home and set apart from family work, the workplace became a man's world! Fathers concentrated on bringing money into the home by their daily absence from it, and mothers concentrated on homemaking and child rearing. In fact, raising almost-perfect children became a critical task for mothers. If women were involved in paid work it was usually done at home or close to home, and often resembled types of work done for their families, such as nursing, sewing, teaching, or housekeeping.

During this same period there was a proliferation of new beginnings for 5 million immigrants who came from literally all over Europe to the United States. Americans have been proud of the "melting pot" that represents U.S. society because of the diversity of people, language, culture, and values that immigrant families brought with them. However, most immigrant families came from peasant and agricultural societies that did not prepare them for life in an industrialized urban society. While immigrants were struggling with the same problems as the native farm families, they had the added obstacles of lack of language competency, conflicting value systems, and conflicting religious imperatives.

In order to "Americanize" all immigrants and to accommodate the "urbanized" farm families, a host of organizations were created that are still very much part of the current social picture: urban school systems, settlement houses, health departments, charitable and welfare agencies, and day nurseries.

Immigrant mothers usually had to work for economic reasons, and the care of young children became a major societal concern. The day nursery movement was one answer to this problem, providing a "relief service" to working mothers. In fact, it is this concept of care for children during periods of crisis that has prevailed in the United States. Child care by someone other than the mother or a close family member has consistently been viewed as a temporary condition to repair breakdowns for families with emergencies, when no other solution could be found. In the *Charities Review Journal* (August 1927) it was noted that "the day nursery movement should be a temporary alternative to child rearing, and primarily a way to allow mothers to work when fathers were either incompetent or unavailable."[3] It was suggested that the day nursery should *not* attempt to save the child by disregarding other family members. Families today are all too familiar with family members, friends, neighbors, and the media who echo the same sentiments as the 1927 *Journal* article: that only in crisis can families allow "outsiders" to help care for their children.

World War I: Conflict and Change

World War I brought not only the problems of involvement in a world war, but also change and conflict for American families. There was the need to adapt to the outside world; there was increased separation of families, and less time for enjoyment together in work and family activities. Once again, there was a reduction in the time that men could be involved in helping to shape the lives of their children. The guiding rule was that marriage was a career for a woman as it never could be for a man.[4] As a result, the following beliefs became firmly entrenched in the definition of the American family:

- A mother's place is in the home, caring for her children and devoting her energy and talent to the family.
- A mother must provide continued, devoted care for her children and be capable of suspending her own needs for the passionate and fragile needs of her child.
- A child's disorderly and chaotic passions continually require a woman to be an expert in child rearing.
- A man must "make it" in the world of work.
- A father needs to turn his attention to gratification achieved away from home.
- A father is uninterested in his young children and less nurturant than a mother.
- The "one right way" to work or to parent is to follow our own parents' path.

World War II:
Women Join the Workforce

World War II's GI Joe and Rosie the Riveter are well known to all. GI Joe was recruited to fight a major world war and Rosie the Riveter was recruited at the workplace, in an attempt to fill the job vacancies left by men who were part of the war effort. In fact, the sense of emergency surrounding the war effort relaxed the social pressures for the employment of married women with children. Female participation in the paid labor force was at an all-time high! According to a *Time* magazine article in 1943, women were expected to assume work roles outside the home as part of their patriotic duty. Employers were told by the U.S. War Manpower Commission not to set up any barriers to employment for women with children, and were urged to arrange flexible working hours and work shifts to help mothers coordinate work and family.

As World War II ended, many GI Joes returned home, and a frequent postwar cry was, "Mothers return home." However, Rosie the Riveter and many of her friends did not return to their role as traditional homemakers. The nation had a desire to return to normalcy, but many women continued to work in paid employment for economic reasons; because of separation, death, or desertion of a spouse; or because of desire and satisfaction. In addition, the unexpected expansion of the economy after World War II plus the low birth rate in the period from 1930 to 1945 created a labor shortage that provided married women with an atmosphere that was more sympathetic to their need and desire to work outside the home. Employers, husbands, and some women agreed that it was okay for women to work at a paid job—*if* it did not interfere with their work at home. Thus we see that the seeds for the Superperson tension often felt by wives today were sown in the postwar era. The notion of shared responsibility was yet to come to the forefront.

The 1950s Ideal: Recapturing the Past

After the long periods of separation, isolation, insecurity, and emotional and social starvation that had been fueled by the Great Depression, two world wars, and vast changes in values and lifestyles, there was a great need for American families of the 1950s to attempt to recapture a romanticized past in which home and hearth were dominant.

Americans seemed eager to retreat to their personal lives and forget the pain that they had suffered during long periods of conflict. Women were reminded that it was time to turn their energy inward to the family. Popular women's magazines gave advice to young married women that reflected the tone of the time:

- Be unselfish. Put yourself second.
- Any thoughtful woman can find ways to express herself. But she should not neglect her role as a wife.
- The happy wife adapts her mood to fit her husband's. She hides her own disappointments. If she's arranging the living room, she'll put the big chair by the fire where he wants it even though it spoils the effect she planned.
- A woman should remain in the background and provide for her family's needs and comforts.

Additional advice about "proper" male and female roles and family structures was offered to families via the popular culture, books of the time, everyone's daily newspaper, and local and state public affairs reports:

- Plainly this nation needs a father in the armchair at the head of the table again, carving the roast, disciplining the children, keeping the peace, settling disputes, loving his wife but reserving his pants for his own use, serving as an example for sons to emulate and daughters to seek in husbands.[5]
- Home should be father's castle. When it's just his barracks, can you blame him for going A.W.O.L.?[6]

- However good it may be for father to take some responsibility for domestic work, we must resist at all points the increasingly popular notion that the father and mother should have equal responsibility. Not only is this unfair to the hard-working man; it is far more unfair to the woman. . . . If we take from the mother the notion that she is the queen of her little kingdom, we are taking away her most legitimate source of pride, we are adding to her frustration, and we are harming the total family life.[7]

The social ideal that emerged during the 1950s still haunts us today. Many of you were children in the 1950s, reared by parents who were part of an idealized family life. If you are the parent of young children today you were probably raised to believe that the patterns of family life you witnessed in the 1950s and 1960s were typical of the entire twentieth century and the "one right way." In fact, the only model that you as a parent have probably had to follow is the one you were reared with. Your parents were part of a generation that popularized middle-class values, the idea of living in a vine-covered cottage with a picket fence and flowers in bloom. Living well in suburbia, and "having it all," meant that fathers would work long hours to earn money and mothers would keep everything in the house running smoothly, making their children and their children's needs the most significant part of their lives. Children in fact monopolized most of mother's lives. Peter Drucker writes that during this period in history it became the mark for a self-respecting man that his wife need not work for wages. Drucker, in a *Wall Street Journal* article, states that until 20 years ago, "female emancipation largely meant freeing women from the necessity of taking a paying job."[8]

A woman in Iowa told of her own father's attitude toward working women, an attitude that mirrors Drucker's perception of the 1950s working man:

My mother was a typical housewife until my youngest brother was in second grade. I was 12. She had worked before I was born, as a secretary, then as a Kelly Girl, part time—on and off—much to my father's dismay, since he thought mothers should stay home and look like they didn't really need to work.

Whether your parents experienced the idyllic lifestyle presented, or only fantasized about it, one must remember that they believed it; believing it made it right and so we have a whole generation of grandparents who now tell the parents of today:

- Our children were everything to us. Why, we never went out without them! How can you leave those children to go to work?
- I'm sad that you're not home with the children all the time. I have the same sadness about your sisters. In my heart I believe that the one best way for mothers is to be at home all the time.

Beth Gibbons (first introduced in Chapter 2) expressed her frustration about the same subject:

Jack's mother—she never gives her opinion much—but she's made it clear, in an indirect way. She tells me about other women and says, "Can you believe she takes her baby to a babysitter? I would not allow anyone to care for my children except their mother."

Another frustrating but poignant story on the subject of a mother's role was told to us by one of the families interviewed:

I had gone out to a professional meeting, leaving my two-year-old son and three-year-old daughter with my parents and my husband. When I returned home, all was quiet except for my mother, who was furious with me but with little explanation of the reason. I checked with my husband, and he told me that while I was gone our two-year-old son, while "dancing" to the music on his record player, fell and was injured. My husband and father rushed our child to the emergency room and were greeted by our pediatrician, who swiftly attended to the matter at hand, and then hours later told my husband how fortunate we were because the injury could have been fatal. For this, my mother was furious with me, and her comments were, "How could you go to a meeting and leave your baby?" Three adults—father, grandfather, and grandmother—could not care for two children; only mother could do it.

When one examines the beliefs and traditions of an earlier generation, it is not difficult to see why so many contemporary mothers and fathers are haunted by the voices of the past.

Work and the Family in Contemporary America: "The Subtle Evolution"

There are times when a generation is caught . . . between two ages, two modes of life, with the consequence that it loses all power to understand itself and has no standards, no security, no simple acquiescence.

—Herman Hesse
Steppenwolf

The past two decades have been labeled the period of "the subtle revolution." This "subtle revolution" has really been a "subtle evolution" and had its roots in preindustrial America. Patterns of work and family have been in transition throughout the history of our nation. The American family and workplace have moved from an agricultural society to an industrial society and currently to an information-processing society. This evolution has followed families from rural communities to urban communities to suburban communities; we are now witnessing families moving back to urban and rural communities. Families have survived periods of economic depression, prosperity, recession, and inflation. There have been periods of world wars, periods between wars, periods of increased birthrates and decreased birthrates, and periods of turbulence and tranquility. Through periods of crisis and necessity both men and women have abandoned or exchanged traditional roles. All of this has created change within what has always been termed the "typical" American family.

Accompanying this change has been its inevitable companion: conflict. Conflict between what we accepted before and what we believe in now. Conflict, as Donald Bell notes in *Being a Man: The Paradox of Masculinity*,[9] between "old ways and new, between the era in which we grew up and the time in which we now live." Conflict between our emotional beliefs, rooted in the past, and our intellectual convictions, a product of the present. This conflict comes as much from within ourselves as from the outside world.

The conflict we feel is revealed in our actions and words. Carla Pierson, co-owner of several successful franchise operations with her husband Mark, describes her experiences:

> See, what's really happened for me is that I get a real strong mother instinct from my mother, the Super Mother. But I have very strong instincts from my father, the Successful Businessman. And I go through my days feeling schizophrenic.

Carla's ambivalence is not unusual. Joan and Mark Miller (first introduced in Chapter 2) also discussed how underlying beliefs rooted in the past color their attitudes and actions in the present. Joan, for example, is concerned that her father thinks that "Mark isn't a real man because his primary motivation isn't making money." Consequently, she sometimes feels that Mark should attend more to his career responsibilities, even if this comes at the expense of his family responsibilities.

Stresses and strains are to be expected when our lives are characterized by change and conflict. As a result, we do not understand ourselves all the time; and as Hesse noted, we lack self-comprehension. We often express surprise and disappointment at our state of conflict. We sometimes catch ourselves yearning for simpler times of less change and diminished conflict.

As the Generation with Choices, we must learn to accept our divided feelings as normal. We need to focus our energies on examining the personal, societal, and cultural roadblocks that inhibit us—and unleashing our creative energies to overcome them!

4

Beware: Work/Family Roadblocks Ahead!

I shall be telling this with a sigh
Somewhere ages and ages hence:
Two roads diverged in a wood, and I—
I took the one less traveled by,
And that has made all the difference.

—Robert Frost
"The Road Not Taken"

When we interviewed the working parents for this book, we were impressed with their strength and their concern for the future of their families. We were keenly aware of the differences between those working parents who appeared to be successful in their attempts to balance their careers and their home life, and those who appeared continually stymied by roadblocks in their work/ family lives. Roadblocks, whether they are self-imposed or dic-

34

tated by our culture and society, limit people's choices, their decision making, and ultimately their personal fulfillment and control over their lives.

As families struggle with the roadblocks in their work/family journey, they often have regrets about "roads not taken." Your regrets may be less severe, and you may be able to judge yourself less harshly, if many or all the forks in the road can be explored at the onset of your work/family journey. Being able to identify which options are unrealistic and which ones present personal opportunities and choices for you is a key step toward the successful integration of your career and your family.

You may recall the roadblocks you have encountered as being any of the following:

- Your neighbor won't babysit for you.
- Your husband is going out of town this Friday and won't be available to pick your daughter up at the child-care center.
- Your son's teacher calls you at the office to inform you that, for the third day in a row, Ricky has wet his pants.
- You have more and more trouble getting out of the house on time in the morning.
- You receive this month's bank statement and realize that your last five checks are going to bounce.
- Your child's before- and after-school program is closing this week.
- Your boss wants you to stay late tonight and you can't.
- Your in-home caregiver has called in sick again.
- Your child tells you it's okay, he doesn't mind if you miss the spring carnival at school this Thursday.
- Your vice president for planning has announced that she's pregnant.
- Your best salesperson complains that he can never call in his orders after 3 P.M. because your secretary is always on the phone with her kids.

We recognize how serious any of these dilemmas can appear to you. But when we discuss roadblocks, we have in mind a definition somewhat broader in scope. We are looking not so much at the narrow focus of day-to-day problems you may be facing, but at their foundations, which are embedded within larger issues.

This chapter will address the four major areas in the lives of working parents that most often prevent them from maximizing their personal opportunities for integrating work and family life. With insight into these areas, you can beware of the roadblocks ahead!

Remember that each roadblock presented in this chapter presents problems but also presents opportunities and solutions. Sometimes a roadblock requires only a temporary detour. Sometimes by chance or choice a detour will take you over a new path that enhances your life more than the road you originally thought you wanted. Every roadblock to the merger of work and family can lead you to discover a creative pathway to satisfaction and mastery over your life—*if* you recognize the opportunities hidden within each problem.

Roadblock No. 1: The Nine-Dot Problem at Home and at Work

. . . the human spirit, when freed of ignorance and cant, has remarkable resilience. However bowed and bent it may temporarily seem, it may still throw off its unthinking and conventionalist chains, and rise above handicaps.

—Albert Ellis and Robert A. Harper
A Guide to Rational Living

In introductory psychology courses around the country, students are introduced to a classic conceptual problem: the nine-dot problem. Usually it's presented as a problem of connecting nine cities by straight highways, each section of which must start where the last section stopped. A maximum of four lines is permitted with no repeat construction or retracing of steps. A map of the nine cities is given to the students (see Figure 1) and they begin the assignment.

Inevitably a few students will come up with the right answer, either because they're familiar with the problem or because they're smart enough to ask someone from last year's class. Most

Figure 1. The nine dot problem: map of the nine cities in the proposed U.S. highway system.

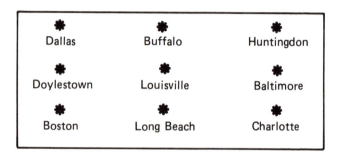

people are stumped. In reality, the nine-dot problem isn't complicated; people make it so. We approach the problem with implicit assumptions that make it impossible to solve. We assume that the solution must fall within fixed boundaries and that those boundaries are defined by the shape of the map. Nothing in the instructions tells us to limit ourselves in this way; we impose the limitations on ourselves, unconsciously or consciously. Until we can free ourselves from our self-imposed boundaries we can't solve the problem. The solution involves going outside the rectangle, as illustrated in Figure 2.

Our Boundaries: Time, Money, and Support

We asked parents, "What are the major obstacles to the merger of work and family? What holds you back from getting what you want?" The answers we repeatedly heard were: time, money, support. Or, more accurately: no time, no money, no support.

Are the three factors mentioned above our real-life version of the boundary assumption in the nine-dot problem? Are these factors intrinsic parameters or artificially constructed bounda-

Figure 2. Possible solution for the nine-dot problem.

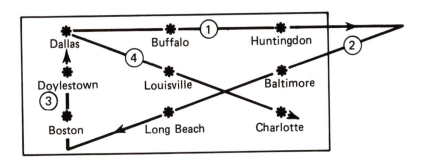

ries to our problem solving? Do we attribute exaggerated importance to them or do we treat them appropriately? As we examine each of the three factors, we will be trying to answer these questions.

Time: The Scarcest Resource

> In reality, time never flies and never drags. It is the most inexorable and inelastic element in our existence. The only constant and totally predictable resource is the availability and movement of time.
>
> —R. Alec Mackenzie and Kay W. Cronkite
> *About Time: A Woman's Guide to Time Management*

Time is a fixed resource. We try to ignore this, and talk of enough and not enough time, of excrutiatingly long seconds and flown-by hours. But the facts remain. Every minute is sixty seconds. Every hour is sixty minutes. Time is a resource we can't manipulate: We can't stretch it or shrink it. We have all of it that we will ever have.

Yet people persist in trying to alter this fact. Dental student Jim Brooks confided that he, like so many others, derives great pleasure from pushing the snooze alarm at least three times every morning.

> Somehow, it makes me feel so good to push that button—to physically press something and say to myself, "Okay, you've got a half an hour" and the "Okay, ten minutes" and then "That's it!" It probably sounds weird, but it's like controlling time.

Controlling time: the ultimate conquest of our scarcest resource. We dream of freezing time, borrowing time, saving time: They are mere illusions. We ask for extensions and time off and overtime. Children beg for "five more minutes," and we act as though we have the power to grant such a request. The five minutes turn into ten more minutes and then a half an hour, and our sense of power is transformed into exasperation. "How much time do you want?" we demand angrily. "As much as I can get," is the unspoken but truthful answer.

What would we do if we were granted this wish for more time? Ignoring for a moment the impossibility of the request, what do we think a greater quantity of time would give us? Some of us think it would allow us greater flexibility, greater freedom, the ability to spend more hours or minutes on the things that are important to us. Such beliefs contradict Parkinson's Law: Work will expand to fill the time available. Lucy MacFarlane, a nurse and mother of a three-year-old son, acknowledged the validity of this natural phenomenon.

> I think that despite my plans to stay home with him and do all those developmental things with him—the truth of the matter is that you don't spend a whole lot of time doing that. When I spent more time at home, I did basically what I see a lot of women at home do—take care of the house, do the chores, watch the kids. And sometimes in that order.

Given the fixed nature of time as a resource, and accepting Parkinson's Law as a reality, we try to devise ways of managing time. We construct elaborate schedules and aspire to efficiency.

In the 1970s, the Superperson was spawned as one answer to our lack of time. Daily routines were established to achieve a perfectly orchestrated, constant rate of activity. The image was supposed to be flawless: meteor-like career advancement, effortless entertaining, sensitive parenting, responsive relationships. The best of the past was to merge with the best of the present to produce the best of the future: The Best Boss, The Best Parent, The Best Employee.

The Superperson knew the value of time and drove a hard bargain. "Well," he chuckled, "if I can't have more, I might as well make the most of what I have!" And so quality time was brought into this world. Its birth announcement read, "It's not how much time you have, but what you do with it." Anxious, frazzled parents rejoiced at such a notion, but their glee was short-lived. Nagging doubts returned, fears of not enough time persisted, and those fears are still a part of our lives. Tom Gonzales, a chief surgical resident, voices them:

> One thing I always think about is the feeling that I'm not getting enough time to spend with Diane [his wife]. Being in this profession means I won't have much time to spend with my family. I suppose that means making the most of my time—quality time, they say—but I wonder if that's not kidding ourselves.

Tom isn't alone in his sentiments. Almost half of the parents surveyed by United Media Enterprises (in a report on leisure in America) in 1983 felt that they were spending too little time with their children.[10] Why do we feel that way, despite findings that indicate employed parents (especially fathers in dual-career families) interact with their children more often than parents in traditional families? It is because time's measurement is largely subjective. Time is a reflection of our values, not of reality. There is no objective scale that determines the right amount of time to spend alone, or working, or with one's spouse, or with one's child.

We won't find the solution to the "not enough time" problem by chasing after more time. The truth is we will never have enough of it and we can never manage it. There is no substitute for it. The most we can do is manage ourselves and our families in relation to time.

In response to our question of how parents achieve this, we were told:

- I've arranged with a woman in town who cooks far better meals than I ever could to prepare dinner for my family two nights a week. I stop by her house on my way home and avoid having to spend my first hour at home madly rushing about trying to be with the kids, make dinner, and unwind.
- It's taken me a while to catch on to this, but I now shop almost exclusively at places that deliver—drugstores, dry cleaning establishments, grocery stores, hardware stores. If you invest a little time up front finding these places, the payoff can be substantial.
- The best gift I ever received was a telephone answering machine. It's like having a built-in secretary at home. I don't feel compelled to answer the phone when I really don't have time to talk.

Tips like this that save you an hour a day—or even less— can add up to make a big difference. The most important key to using your time effectively is to make sure that your time expenditures accurately reflect your values and priorities. Two of the most common causes of time mismanagement are (1) spending too much time on tasks that you claim are unimportant to you, and (2) being overburdened and overextended because you assume total responsibility for too many things. Here is an exercise to help you decide whether one or both of these problems affect you and if so, what you can do about it.

Problem:

Wasting time (spending time on low-priority, unimportant things).

Symptoms:

Self-castigation for:
1. Talking too much on the phone.
2. Excessive unscheduled socializing with unexpected visitors.
3. Spending the last two hours waiting at the TV repair shop, auto mechanic's, and so on.
4. Spending the entire morning at the grocery store when you'd intended to stay only 45 minutes.

Possible Solutions:

1. Don't be a slave to the phone or doorbell. Both were intended to be conveniences, not burdens. You can always:
   a. Buy an inexpensive answering machine for the phone and monitor your calls.
   b. Tell other family members you don't want to be disturbed and ask them to answer the phone or door and take messages.
   c. Request that friends and and family generally call and visit you during specified times (in morning, after dinner, before 10:00 P.M.)
   d. Not answer the phone or door.
2. Teach or request other family members (especially children) to respect your need to be alone or work uninterrupted. A closed door can and should be respected at home as much as it is elsewhere.
3. Avoid "stream of consciousness" behavior in which you start one thing, which leads to another, which leads to another, which leads to another, and so on. Don't clean the sink and then decide you might as well reorganize the cupboards and, as long as you're doing that, mop the floor. *Stick to your intentions.*
4. Invest time and money in preventive car and appliance maintenance. The tire you get fixed now involves far less hassle than the tire you have to get repaired in New York City at 2:00 A.M.

5. Look around for stores that deliver dry cleaning, groceries, pharmaceuticals, and so on to your home and see whether the delivery charge is worth it.
6. Investigate the possibility of hiring (or trading services with) a neighborhood teenager, college student, or retiree to do your errand-hopping.

Problem:

Doing it all (handling more than your share of responsibilities).

Symptoms:

Beliefs such as:
1. "No one can do this as well as I can, let alone better."
2. "I can't burden anyone else with these things, so I'll just have to do them myself." (Martyrdom.)
3. "In the end, I'll get saddled with the task if I want it done right, so I might as well do it from the start."

Possible Solutions:

1. Ask yourself two questions:
    a. Does this task need to be done at all?
    b. Does this task need to be done the way I do it?
    If the task doesn't need to be done, eliminate it. If the task needs to be done but doesn't have to be done your way, delegate it to someone else. If it does need to be done, and for some idiosyncratic reason it *must* be done your way, don't delegate that task. You'll end up criticizing the way the other person does it, or, even worse, doing it over again yourself.
2. Eliminate the supervisory role. Once tasks are delegated by mutual agreement, forget about those things you aren't responsible for.
3. Don't automatically assume a task because you're the only one who knows how to do it. People *are* trainable! Be patient and encouraging.

Money: The Overvalued Resource

H. L. Mencken once said that "the chief value of money lies in the fact that one lives in a world in which it is overestimated."[11]

On the other hand, it's hard to underestimate the value of money. The saying "Money talks" is not without merit. The enormous costs of raising a child to age 18 are sobering. A Conference Board research bulletin reported that in 1980 the direct cost of raising a child in an average family was around $85,000. If opportunity costs and four years of college are added in, the costs increases to a staggering estimated sum of $100,000 to $140,000.[12]

Whether we see money as an expandable or fixed resource determines what we do in response to our constant perception that we don't have enough. If we see money as elastic, then we commence ways to increase our income: joining the workforce, moonlighting, working overtime, changing jobs, buying on credit. If we see money as an unchanging resource, we set out to cut expenses: a cheaper car, a vacation at home or no vacation at all, less meat for dinner. In both cases, we are adjusting the income expense ratio. In both cases, we are assuming that money is a legitimate, inherent boundary. We try to stay within that boundary by pushing it outward or shrinking our expenses to fit inside the concrete line.

The solutions people see to the "not enough money" dilemma are shaped by a fundamental assumption: Only money can buy what we need or want. Money—whether it be in the form of a check, money order, credit card, or cash—is the medium of exchange.

It's undoubtedly true that there is no free lunch. What is doubtful, or at least worth investigating, is the assumption that you have to buy that lunch with money. Historically, money hasn't always been accorded exclusive rights to the market. During colonial times, during the Great Depression, and again during the 1960s, services and goods weren't always purchased. They were exchanged and shared. Resources were extended, either through developing self-sufficiency skills or through barter.

When most of us think of barter, we conjure up images of country doctors getting paid in chickens and tomatoes, and settlers exchanging pelts and wampum with Indians. The range of exchangeable goods and services is much more sophisticated and extensive. Car pooling, babysitting co-ops, food co-ops, agreements along the lines of "I'll do your tax return if you'll fix my furnace"—all of these exchanges take place without money. One of the women we spoke with explained how she and her husband surmounted the seemingly prohibitive cost of a babysitter.

> Jim and I were beginning to feel as though we were prisoners in our own home. Our budget was already straining at the edges and since our family lives 300 miles away, free babysitting was out of the question. Or at least, we thought it was . . . until I heard about a man down the street who was in a bind because he couldn't find any after-school care for his nine-year-old son. We worked out a deal whereby I watch his son two afternoons a week and he babysits for our two kids Friday or Saturday when we go out.

An extension of the bartering process is role sharing, which allows for the planning of activities with not only a spouse or a child, but a friend, relative, neighbor, sitter, or child-care worker.

Diana Tyler, whom you met in Chapter 2, told us that when the circus came to her community she was upset about not being able to take Heather, because Diana was directing a seminar for unwed mothers. Diana could have asked her parents to take Heather to the circus, but instead she asked a colleague to role-share with her. Heather got to the circus, Diana was able to fulfill her obligations at work, and Diana's colleague could look forward to homemade bread for her family for the next few weeks.

Working parents can find financial as well as emotional relief by making a list of individuals who can role-share with them. Some categories to consider when making your list of role-sharing possibilities are:

- Who can share child care with me?

- Who can share home management with me?
- Who can share some categories of job responsibility?
- Who can share commuting?

Bartering services is only one way of getting what we want without spending money. Another is self-help. Over the last 15 or 20 years, there's been a tremendous increase in the number of people who simply elect to do things themselves rather than pay others to fix the car, paint the house, remodel the kitchen, install a shower, and so on. Any library or bookstore has a wide variety of how-to books on virtually every subject imaginable. Also, many high schools, community colleges and universities, recreation centers, and churches have gotten into the market of offering adult education classes, where for a nominal fee you can learn how to tune a car, prepare gourmet meals, make wine, cane chairs, and so on.

Joan Hirsch (introduced in Chapter 2) told us about her experience with self-help when she and Doug purchased a new car.

> All the options—even the smallest things like protective rim around the wheels or along the side of the door—cost a fortune. I could think of a lot of other things I'd like to do with the money, and so I opted for buying trim at a local discount store, reading the directions, and applying it myself.

Support: The Untapped Resource

Families don't exist in isolation, though many have long pretended that they do. The family unit—the nuclear family as a free-standing, self-sufficient entity—is a myth. It inhibits us from tapping a potentially limitless resource: support.

Support can come from ourselves, friends, colleagues, employers, spouses, children, other family members, communities, church groups, professional associations . . . the list continues. It can be emotional, physical, and financial, direct and indirect.

With such a variety of sources, it seems inconceivable that we could be lacking in support. Why are so many families unable to find it? Perhaps a better question would be why so many are *unwilling* to find it.

On the whole, we don't ask for support. Somehow everyone is supposed to know intuitively what we need. To have to *ask* for support, to deliberately seek it out, lessens its value. For example: Jack Gibbons is constantly being taken to task for not realizing what Beth wanted him to say or do. When he asks, "Why didn't you just ask me to make dinner tonight?" the answer is invariably, "I shouldn't *have* to ask." Support, we seem to say, is best when it is given unsolicited.

Our reluctance to seek support is based on more than the wish that people knew what we want. It's rooted in the self-sufficiency myth, the nostalgic vision of the rugged individualist. We don't ask for support because we aren't supposed to need it. The perfect family is an independent family, self-sustaining, self-healing, self-contained. To seek help in any form implies inadequacy or failure.

No wonder that women have been labeled as notoriously poor delegators in the home: Many have believed that they could and should do it alone. Similarly, one of the characteristics of a workaholic is an inability to delegate; how could it be otherwise? Workaholics, symbol of the Protestant work ethic at its extreme, can't rely on others. They have to do everything themselves to be sure it's done right.

Our barriers to seeking support are not all of our own making, however. By contrast to many other cultures, American society is fragmented and highly mobile. Bryant Robey, in his book *The American People*, tells us that almost half of all Americans five years and older in 1980 moved at least once during the preceding five years.[13] Even if we asked for support, would it readily be there? In a society where friends come and go, sisters and brothers live on opposite coasts, parents retire to faraway states, and about 40 percent of marriages end in divorce before the fifteenth anniversary, how can we believe that support is there for the asking?

Often we experience intense feelings of isolation and alienation. Laurie Brown described to us the difficulties of her first year in law school:

I was really desperate. I felt like there was nobody there who cared about my kids or my family problems. There just wasn't anybody I could really talk to that cared about the difficulties of meshing a professional career with the problems of raising very young children.

For all these reasons, we have tended to turn inward for support. Feelings of isolation, pride, and fear of weakness have combined to produce a false barrier to our exploration of this resource. Unlike time and money, which we seek more of and try to maximize through management, support remains an untapped resource.

This is surprising in light of the fact that as children, many of us were members of groups such as Little League, the Scouts, ballet class, school choir, or drama club—groups that encouraged us to expand our circle of relationships. Yet as working parents, we tend to retreat into the confines of our nuclear family—and then bemoan the fact that we lack support!

Although you may not choose to purchase a large Victorian house to share with other nuclear families (as Donna and Michael Mayo did, described in Chapter 2), you can extend your support system in a number of ways:

- Form your own support group, if necessary, as Laura did when she sought out other first-year law students who were parents.
- Ask your employer to consider the possibility of sponsoring working parent seminars during lunch hour. (We will discuss this in more detail in Chapter 6).
- Contact a senior citizens center and see whether there's any interest in establishing a foster grandparents program. Or suggest to your child's teacher the possibility of setting up an intergenerational program that will give your child and senior adults the opportunity to interact with one another. (See Appendix C for the names and addresses of intergenerational programs.)

Getting Beyond the Nine-Dot Problem

Lack of time, money, or support becomes a major roadblock to parents when they assume that what is familiar and visible is all that's available. The part-time employee may find that reduced work hours don't mean reduced overall workload or salary. The budding barterer may be pleasantly surprised to discover that the couple upstairs doesn't mind occasional babysitting if in exchange the front walk gets shoveled. The parent deciding about the possibility of joint custody can learn the pros and cons according to the experts—parents who are actually doing it. There are many possibilities for detours around the resource roadblock if we have the imagination to challenge our assumptions about where our boundaries really lie.

Roadblock No. 2: The Search for Perfection and Single Answers

The art of living does not consist in preserving and clinging to a particular mode of happiness, but in allowing happiness to change its form without being disappointed by the change; for happiness, like a child, must be allowed to grow.

—Charles Langbridge Morgan

In Aesop's fables there is a story of a donkey who starved to death because he was equally distant from two identical bales of hay and couldn't decide between them. The donkey wanted to make the perfect choice and searched for the single best answer. He wanted the perfect bale of hay, but he deliberated too much and too long, and unfortunately it was too late for any choice at all.

The moral of the story for the working parent may be that looking too hard for the single best answer to problems at home and at work can immobilize you instead of freeing you to take creative action toward satisfying the balance of work and family life. We have all been conditioned to search for perfection and

51

single answers in a world that is ever changing, laden with probability and chance, and therefore uncertain and imperfect.

Our Culture Emphasizes Perfection

The American culture has been referred to as a "driven culture" that stresses achievement, competition, and perfection. Ever since the first immigrants came to this country in search of a better society and unlimited opportunity, Americans have been conditioned to expect a great deal from themselves and from society. As mentioned earlier, our culture has taught us that the perfect father is one who identifies himself through his job. He is taught to work hard, to assure financial support for his family, and, as Donald Bell notes in his book *Being a Man: The Paradox of Masculinity,* "to always be strong, dominant, and competent."[14] The perfect mother has been taught to be a reservoir of energy, devotion, availability, accommodation, and charm, and to identify herself through her home and family.

In addition to the perfect father and perfect mother, corporate America has traditionally believed in the perfect employee. Perfect employees make work their major concern and define themselves through their jobs, often at the expense of intimacy and personal relationships.

The expectations and acceptable rules of society have been carved out of traditional patterns of work and family life that are no longer applicable to current societal conditions. As stated in Chapter 2, we are now in a time of transition; the interface of work and the family is unique and complex. The profound changes among contemporary American families make it impossible for these families to be guided by the same societal rules that guided their parents.

Ironically, many working parents, in struggling to define their new role, have simply combined the old images into one of Superperson—the perfect parent *and* the perfect employee, all rolled into one. By achieving perfection not just in one area of their lives, but in several simultaneously, they can have it all.

It's one thing to dream of perfection, but expecting ourselves to achieve it dooms us to feelings of inadequacy and creates roadblocks to the realistically successful merger of work and family. The workplace constructs roadblocks when employers demand exclusive loyalty to one's job. Roadblocks are also constructed when people believe there is one best way to be successful as a parent or at one's job, or that the only acceptable sex roles are those that have been decided on by one's ancestors.

The Search for the Perfect Parent

"My husband applauds my accomplishments as a wife and mother; my employer has rewarded my accomplishments by promoting me three times in the last two and a half years. So, if everyone thinks I'm so successful, why do I feel so awful so much of the time?" lamented one mother in our interview group. Kim Greenspan and her husband Carl talked at length about their personal experiences as parents, as employees, and as son and daughter. Most of all, they spoke of Kim's expectations for a Madonna-like perfection in every aspect of her life. Kim reiterated more than once:

> No one ever tells us [parents] all the facts. It's only recently that people are talking openly and honestly to each other about their feelings on parenting, about their successes, their failures, their doubts. Up to now, mothers felt that unless we devoted ourselves 100 percent to caring for others, we were selfish. We weren't supposed to find satisfaction in areas unrelated to the care and nurturing of our family.

Kim recalled "the most horrible experience of my life":

> I came home from work and was greeted as usual by my two children. It was an especially difficult day at work, but rewarding too; I had completed a major project. I was met

at the door by my two bright-eyed, beautiful children. Normally this greeting was enough to perk me up, but not that day. I was exhausted and the children seemed more energetic than usual.

My body said, ''Let the children amuse themselves and you sit down, put your feet up, and relax.'' However, my mind insisted, ''You must spend time with the children.'' I gave in to my emotions regarding my children. After all, what mother wouldn't want to spend time with her children, especially when that mother has been gone all day at her job?

My answer to the problem was, give them a bath. It's relaxing, it's fun, and they must have one before they go to bed anyhow. Toys, bubbles, splashing about, just the thing. I filled the bath with water, put the two children into the tub, and sat down on the edge of the tub. I watched them splash around for a bit and then without warning the most overwhelming feeling of panic and terror gripped me. I felt weak and terribly frightened. I pulled the plug from the bathtub to allow the water to go out, (always thinking— even in my panic) and literally ran from the bathroom to the telephone. I called Carl at his office, insisted he come home immediately, and hung up.

Carl rushed home expecting the worst. He found two children amusing themselves and one very distraught mother. Carl took charge for the next few hours. With the children being cared for, I attempted to take stock of the horror I had experienced. Please understand, not all my answers were evident at once, but enough answers did surface in order for me to evaluate my experience.

Kim and Carl indicated that in retrospect, their story was probably not at all different from those of other parents. Kim's extreme response of terror and pain came from not knowing that other parents have bad days, from self-imposed pressure to achieve perfection both at home and at work, and from feelings of inadequacy experienced by many working parents who are trying to have it all. As Kim explained,

I was terrified of my thoughts, thoughts that I hadn't shared with anyone. I really didn't want to be the perfect mother that day. It would have been nice not to come home to two children that day. Would I harm the two most precious people in my life? Is this the way child abuse starts? Why am I so terrible? Perhaps working and parenting are really not possible.

Carl echoed, "Parenting is always idealized. We can often accept a bad day at the office, but not at home with our family. No wonder parents feel so much guilt."

Parents have constantly tested their effectiveness against the ideal of the perfect parent espoused by the popular press, by their own parents, and by their friends and neighbors. Too few people, magazine articles, or T.V. programs tell working parents that it's okay *not* to be the perfect parent, and to have doubts and regrets at times. Children change often and so dramatically in their first years, and parental responses change in response. Parents are bound to feel both good and bad about parenting through each new stage.

The Double-Edged Sword

Combine the need for perfect parenting with a need to be a perfect employee as defined by you and your employer, and you have a double-edged sword—feelings of inadequacy both on the home front and at work. Nowhere is this better illustrated than in the case of Marie Safford, a 34-year-old corporate attorney who, after two unsuccessful attempts at child-care leaves, decided to resign from her firm. Marie saw herself as a trailblazer. She was the first female attorney hired by a group of lawyers specializing in corporate litigation. After four and a half years on the job, Marie decided to become pregnant. As her due date approached, she sat down with the firm's partners and requested a four-month unpaid maternity leave. Her request was denied, and a compromise unpaid leave of two months was agreed upon. Marie and the firm's partners also agreed that regular and open communication would be necessary during the leave so that business would be minimally disrupted. Marie told us:

> That's where I made my first mistake. The day after my daughter was born, I got a call at the hospital about a brief I was working on. Even though the work wasn't urgent, I was given the impression that I should get it finished as soon as possible. And because I was so conscientious, so afraid that if I appeared the slightest bit negligent in my work that it would hurt me and every other woman who would come after me, I asked my husband to bring all my materials to the hospital. I stayed up almost all night working on it and sent it to the firm the same day I went home from the hospital.

The pattern repeated itself persistently, and at the end of Marie's two-month leave, she felt as though she'd never had a leave at all.

What went wrong? Obviously, Marie and the firm did not effectively communicate their needs to each other. Marie was fearful that too many demands would label her a less than perfect employee. The firm found it easier to pay lip service to Marie's needs than to try to meet them. For a while, the agreement was tolerated. But when the same problem surfaced during a second child-care leave, Marie's frustration and resentment built in a crescendo. Her unsatisfied needs were expressed in her resignation, which came as a shock to the firm. Since Marie's resignation, the firm's ongoing attempts to persuade her to return have been unsuccessful.

The combination of feelings of inadequacy at home and at work may yield responses such as those that Kim and Carl and Marie shared with us. Even if their responses are not quite so dramatic, certainly parents feel anxious and imperfect too much of the time.

The Search for the Perfect Employee

Do perfect employees pay a high price for success? In the traditional "challenge-success model" for career development, employers put a premium on highly productive work during the first five years of employment. This has fostered specific rules of conduct for employees and specific modes of behavior at the workplace in order for an individual to succeed. The implications for workers have been that if you follow the rules, whether they are spoken or unspoken, you will perhaps be rewarded by the organization. Rules beneficial to the organization have not always been beneficial to the employee, who is an individual outside the organization with an emotional and personal life in need of nourishment and development.

The rules for corporate success, as gleaned from numerous readings and interviews with working parents, include:

1. Long hours on the job are crucial.
2. Work as hard as you can, especially in the first five years.
3. Travel when and where the corporation feels it is necessary, regardless of its effect on your family.
4. Present 100 percent commitment to the organization, even if this is at the expense of your family and community.
5. *Never* bring your family concerns, problems, or issues to the office; it's not appreciated and could probably hurt your career in the long run.
6. If you have a spouse, it is understood that your job is more important than his or hers.
7. Always concentrate on what Michael Maccoby in his book *The Gamesman* calls "qualities of the head" and not on "qualities of the heart."[15] Qualities of the head include initiative, pride in performance, and self-confidence; qualities of heart include compassion, generosity, and friendliness. In other words, ignore your feelings and commit yourself to hard work.

8. Relocate without concern for family needs.

You may have more rules to add to this list, depending on the expectations of your own employer.

It's reasonable for organizations to expect hard work and competence, but it's unrealistic for them to ignore the fact that employees also have feelings and personal lives. As one working parent told us:

> There needs to be a recognition that the employee is not a well-oiled machine, always there, ready for everybody at 8:30 A.M. An employee is a person who functions independently from the corporate world. Allowing employees to do work at home—allowing men time to be with families—is crucial. I hope we're going to see across the United States a greater emphasis on the need to really establish a working relationship between employer and employee, not just a game of let's pretend.

Similar responses were voiced by hundreds of working parents as they talked about the exploitive strategies utilized by corporate America to achieve the protection and success of the organization. From a controller in Cedar Rapids, Iowa, we heard:

> Working men and women need to start speaking up—to express their frustrations, their problems, and the way they need help. Working parents and the organization have a responsibility to work together.

A physician spoke of the inconsistency within the pediatric hospital where he works:

> The hospital allows fathers the day off for the birth of their babies and then says, "Well, you can have the day off, but you won't get paid." Ironic, isn't it!

How Corporate America Reinforces the Concept of the Perfect Employee

Employers, until recently, have continued to maintain an image of the American worker that was part of the traditional and idealized typical family portrait of the 1950s. An idealized description of the typical American family can be found in Whyte's 1950s classic *The Organization Man.*[17] There in "Park Forest," Illinois, was the perfect employee that many CEOs use as their model of the ideal employee. This typical worker had a wife who stayed home caring for two children, possibly awaiting the birth of a third child. "Coffee pots bubbled all day long" while wives waited anxiously for their spouses to return home. Park Forest was a homogeneous place constructed from rigid rules, rigid thinking, and rigid responses. Park Forest employees adhered to the rules of the organization. That was all that was thought to be necessary. But was it?

It is ironic that even when corporate America became fascinated by Theory Z and Japanese models for productivity, it ignored one of the keys to Japan's success: security for all employees and provisions for the well-being of their families.

Many working parents feel that businesspeople—often intent on Dow Jones averages, bottom-line considerations, and takeover clashes—have barely recognized the tensions that exist for working parents in attempting to merge work and family life. In accordance with the long-established rules of the business game, many employees are reluctant to share their family concerns with employers because their response is often similar to this one, given to a working parent by her employer:

> We're not in the baby business or the family business, and until that becomes our business, you'll have to work out your personal problems on your own.

Such rigid, impersonal thinking creates obstacles not only for working parents but for the corporations themselves. Many working parents are talented employees! When corporations insist that all their employees follow a single set of organizational rules, they are only lowering morale and productivity, and alienating a growing proportion of the workforce. Setting up roadblocks for working parents is not the way people *or* corporations survive. (This idea is explored further in Chapter 6.)

The Search for the Single Answer

The search for single answers, for the one best way, creates a single-mindedness that prevents working parents from exploring all aspects of their lives. It encourages parents to indulge in a way of thinking they learned as children: either/or.

Either/or thinking helps us make decisions quickly while we maintain reasonable expectations of having chosen correctly. To a certain extent, it makes the decision-making process a fait accompli. In the either/or world, we have little need to deliberate and even less room for self-doubt. We emit sighs of relief as we are spared the stresses of ambiguity.

Certainly either/or has its place in our lives, especially for simple, routine decisions. The problem for many of us and our families emerges when we binge on either/or and forget all the possibilities for creating *ands*. We start feeling trapped by overly simplistic options, neither of which satisfies us. Your needs *or* my needs. Success *or* failure. Father *or* chemist. Mother *or* physician. Work *or* family.

Karen Vandy, an attorney and single mother, recalled for us her first lesson in the either/or approach to work and family.

> I remember when I was in sixth grade I was in a debate. When I finished, my history teacher came up to me and told me that I did a really good job and that I should seriously consider following in my father's footsteps. She thought I would have a good future in law. And I thought my father would be really happy to hear that . . . that he would be really proud of me. And I remember going home

and telling him, and he said, *"Absolutely not!* No daughter of mine is ever going to grow up to be a lawyer. Not if you want a family. You have to make a choice . . . you can't take some man's place in law school and then piddle away your profession.''

What has been neglected in the education and socialization of both sexes is the knowledge that *all* individuals are highly capable of participating in a full range of behaviors that includes both working and parenting. To deny men and women the right to explore all facets of their lives is to diminish their effectiveness as human beings. People who seek single answers forget that children leave the nest and people leave their jobs. If, at age 50 or 60, people feel abandoned, isolated, or unfulfilled, it's often because society's message has been: father *or* electrician, mother *or* nurse.

Would it not be more constructive if people felt that, although they didn't have it all, their bank of self-interest allowed them to make deposits to and withdrawals from both work and family? That way, in the final analysis, they would be left with a positive balance of satisfaction. Being left with a lifetime of withdrawals for regrets about the work/family journey not well traveled will only leave you with an empty emotional bank book.

There are signs that the old pattern of single answers is starting to change. In *Lifeprints: New Patterns of Love and Work for Today's Women,* the authors indicate that ''fewer [marriage] doors are slamming today. A new view of marriage is one that sees the institution as a territory to be occupied, not to be abandoned.'' Marriage, according to Grace Baruch, Rosalind Barnett, and Caryl Rivers, is being ''perceived as a more flexible institution that can change to accommodate both partners. More and more, Americans may be constructing their own marriages rather than accepting old patterns and roles.''[18]

In constructing very individualized marriages and relationships, people will not alienate themselves as workers or parents. In fact, fathers we talked to indicated that the most destructive alienation has been in not allowing men to explore their emotional responses. One father from Minnesota told us:

I think there are a significant number of men who would want to stay at home part of the time and help rear their children, but for the expectation on society's part. It's not a high priority with me what others think; but on the other hand, it's certainly true that's not a completely honest statement because you_ *always* have in the back of your mind what your role is *supposed to be* and how you're working against the tide.

Another father in California said:

We read a good deal about Type A and Type B personalities, stress and its effects on health, men and the risk of heart attacks, but very little about the emotional side of men. Society continues to demand that men explore only one aspect of their lives, that of providing financial support for their families.

A father's reaction to the sole breadwinner role was:

I don't think I'm built to take all the pressure. My own father was a sick man, the result of always feeling the pressure of feeding an entire family. He became sick with the pressure, and my mother never provided any financial support. He never felt he had any choice, and at the time, I suppose he didn't.

Another father declared his frustration over taking time to look beyond the single answer as he explored another dimension of his maleness:

I was told by one career counselor—a Ph.D. from Princeton—"Well, one thing, don't ever tell anyone you spent all that time as a househusband. You'll never get a job." Initially when I went to parties I would carefully gauge the group, particularly if they were older and more conservative. When they asked me what I did, I would tell them, "I am a doctoral candidate." If it was a liberal group I'd say, "I'm a househusband." If it was *real* liberal I'd say,

"I'm a kept man." (Chuckles.) What is needed to dispel the myth of the perfect husband and make the househusband situation work is security in self—a stable self-image and a very stable relationship that consists of not being over-demanding, and where each knows what is expected of the other person.

A contemporary father felt strongly about the need for fathers to share in the parenting of their children. He expressed passionate emotions about his role.

Fathers are pregnant too—many people don't realize it. I make a conscious effort to arrange quality time with my child. Women are often possessive about raising children. Men need and want to be involved too. My choice is not to parent through a woman; I want to define my own role—not to work off any stereotypes, and I don't want to be a mother surrogate. We [fathers] want to be involved. Fathering is easy; parenting is hard. I want to have my own identity—that of a father who is a good parent.

Renee Magid and her husband, David recently had the opportunity to explore the questions and issues relating to the search for a single answer as they marked one of the significant events in their lives, the marriage of their first-born child, Melissa. This experience provided an opportunity for the Magids to examine their responses to the search for single answers. Renee recalls:

While the day was filled with much emotion, feelings of joy, satisfaction, happiness, and optimism, it was also filled with some sadness, for things not completed, trips not taken, experiences unexplored, for precious time that was gone forever. This was also a time for remembering such well-worn phrases as "quality of life," for reexamining decisions made through a lifetime of child rearing—and, most of all, for sharing love and our innermost thoughts about our life together.

As we finally sat down at the conclusion of the wedding and attempted to quell the queazy feelings in our hearts and stomachs, we talked about the past, present, and future. David and I were both struck by some important thoughts. David talked about missing too many events in the children's lives—about the conflicting demands of loyalty to one's job and loyalty to one's family. He talked about his joy and his happiness in watching our son and daughter grow into wonderful human beings. Together we remembered the beginning of our marriage, of feeling different from many of our friends and peers as we attempted to blend all aspects of our lives. We laughed about how I felt like a freak when I would come home from a day of school and other mothers would be sitting on their front porch, infants and toddlers close by. We laughed a lot at this wedding. We cried too.

A large measure of our parenting was over, and up to now our journey had been a successful one. Parenting for both of us was and will probably be one of the most creative endeavors we've devoted ourselves to. However, we were grateful for having explored all aspects of our lives, that we had nurtured our children, ourselves, each other, and our careers. Now with our son and daughter embarking on their own careers, David and I could embark on a new journey. While we would always be parents and would remain married to each other, we were also individuals, with interests shared and careers to continue to develop. I remember thinking that this blending of our roles in no way diminished our satisfaction on this, our daughter's wedding day, and in no way diminished our marriage or our parenting. In fact, it heightened it! We didn't have it all, but we had invested in both our work and family and we felt good! The search for a single answer to our lives may in fact make our lives less fulfilled.

Continual searching for perfection and single answers to complicated issues dooms us to failure, because perfection and single answers do not exist in a complex society. The world we now live in is filled with challenge and change. Even if you are fortunate enough to achieve perfection for a brief period, remaining constantly at this limitless peak is impossible. The long-distance runner may have achieved perfection today as the Number One athlete, but we all know that tomorrow brings a new race, a new challenge, and a new champion. The real world, whether it be work or family, consists of change, imperfection, and fallible human beings.

Working parents who can free themselves of the need for single answers and for perfection at every turn may find it possible to be more creative as they attempt to balance the two most important areas of their lives—their families and their work.

Roadblock No. 3: Failing to Plan

People don't plan to fail;
They fail to plan.

—Popular saying

Jean Sparkin is the mother of a four-year-old daughter, the wife of an attorney, and a paid worker at three different but related jobs. When we asked her whether she did a good deal of personal planning, she quickly replied by nodding her head in an affirmative gesture and pulling a pocket calendar out of her handbag. The calendar revealed to us that just about every block in every week of the month was filled with reminders of appointments, people to call, and hundreds of notes about things to get done. Many working parents are similar to Jean in that they also believe that by keeping a record of their daily schedule, they are in fact doing personal planning.

Jean's diary of events is a written record that could help her in her planning, but right now only serves as a constant reminder to Jean of how frenetic her life is and how little time she has for all her tasks, thus reinforcing her assumption that she is not successful. Jean's pocket calendar does not really help her plan her personal life; it doesn't even help her decide which tasks are important to her—which of the hundreds of listed daily events are helping her make progress with both her work and family life. Nor does it help her to feel any personal satisfaction.

Planning is not simply logging a schedule of events; it is an orderly process that should help you, no matter what the circumstances are, to be relatively sure what the outcome will be. Planning also helps you reduce premature decision making and lower the probability of numerous daily chance events pulling the rug out from under you and making you feel incompetent. Planning can be viewed as a personal road map for success. It helps direct you to your future toward the fulfillment of your goals.

People do think about their goals as they ask themselves familiar questions:

- Will I be the head of the department in the next five years?
- Will my children be successful in school?
- Will my children be happy and productive adults?
- Will I be able to manage two children instead of one?

Planning helps answer such questions so that you can make fantasy a reality.

Life Should Not Be a Mystery

A CEO in Chicago reminisced about his family and an earlier time as he commented about the perceptions people have about planning:

> When my children were very young, we had a favorite game we played on long car trips. It was called the "Mystery Bus Ride." We would give the children little or no information about our plan, and they would, after many questions and answers, attempt to guess where our ultimate destination was. The game usually took up a good deal of time, which of course was our intent, and the interesting thing was that often the children never guessed the right answer. This allowed us to keep the game going over many miles of many trips. Of course, the point here is that the "Mystery Bus Ride" was only a game.

Unless they too are on a mystery journey, most people planning a trip would not leave their plans to chance. They would want to maximize their choices and the outcomes. They would probably ask themselves many or all of the following questions in order to ensure that their journey would be successful:

- Where do I *really* want to go?
- How much emotional and financial investment am I willing to put into this journey?
- What are my priorities in terms of time, energy, interest, and activities?
- What seems right for me based on my current knowledge, information, and resources?

People often respond to statements about personal planning with a grunt, signifying distaste for the process. For many, systematic personal planning is difficult because they associate the process with the structured organization and adherence to time, rules, and regulations they experience in their work life. Personal planning is often viewed as a means of limiting our options, preventing spontaneity and flexibility and providing a programmed approach to family life. As Margaret Coffey (one of the entrepreneurs introduced in Chapter 2) told us, "Rational people plan their paid work lives all the time, because the world of work expects this to be done, but personal planning is often a real problem for people."

Personal planning is systematic but not dogmatic. It helps you take charge of your own life and eliminates the feeling expressed by so many working parents of being out of control. Personal planning provided positive results for those individuals we talked with who incorporated the process into their business and personal lives.

Margaret and Calvin Coffey practice personal planning as the result of on-the-job training and Margaret's formal education in the planning process. When Calvin was planning for the start-up of the family business and Margaret was completing her

M.B.A. at Harvard, both Margaret and Calvin sat down and took a hard look at what they wanted for the future of their family and their work lives. In fact, Margaret told us,

> We actually put together a 150-page plan to address the following issues:
>
> - What kind of people do we enjoy being with?
> - Where do we want to live?
> - What kind of lifestyle do we want for ourselves and our children?
> - How do we define quality of life?
> - What place can meet the needs of both adults?
> - Where can we maximize the success of our new business?
> - Where can we maximize our career plans?
> - How much financial security do we need to be happy?
> - What kind of paid work do we want to be involved with for the next five to ten years?

Calvin commented about the need for personal planning:

> Many people questioned the validity of our ultimate decision, but our plan has paid off. As it turns out, our family business is strategically located, for the area is fast becoming a center for boating. Our plan is working as we expected, and most important, the quality of our lives is what we hoped for.

Another parent applauded the concept of planning in her personal life:

> Use planning to evaluate your financial situation and find out what is available in the community, what kinds of support systems are out there, what child care is available, what fits in with your needs and what you imagine your child's needs will be—and what you'll fall back on if the ideal type of care isn't out there. You need to make yourself educated

and be an aware consumer. Otherwise you may find yourself continually upset, frustrated, and angry.

Personal planning lightens the load for people. It helps them recognize all their options and know where they are going, how to get there, and what they can expect the outcome to be.

Some individuals we met with, instead of planning, fantasized a good deal about how their lives could be. An executive from Chicago told us of her recurring fantasy:

> I can see myself having time for holing up with a carton of good books, quarts of Chinese food, and absolutely no interruptions.

A father from a dual-career family team said:

> I can imagine having time to be together with my spouse—a quiet place, with no telephone, children howling, or constant demands on our schedule.

These people took for granted that the fantasy they longed for would remain just that, a fantasy—something quite unattainable or even unreasonable. They did not recognize the possibilities open to them by incorporating personal planning into their lives. Certainly, a 150-page plan such as the one the Coffeys prepared is not necessary for most people in order to assure a smooth work/family journey, but what is necessary is some realistic and systematic approach to personal planning.

Planning to Be a Planner

If you are unaccustomed to personal planning and are not sure how to begin or how to adapt your business planning to your personal life, then the planning process that follows can be helpful to you. If at the outset the process appears very linear in nature, it is because that is the simplest way to explain it. However, we recognize that the real world, where events often occur at the speed of a rocket, is anything but simplistic and linear! Once you learn sound planning methods, however, they can be applied to many complex and nonlinear situations.

The personalized planning process involves seven steps:

Step 1: Know thyself. Clarify your personal value system.

Step 2: Assess the situation. Think about your current situation at home and at work, and consider all the factors that have an impact on these two areas.

Step 3: Establish your personal goals. Determine what you *really* want to accomplish at home and at work.

Step 4: Put an action plan into motion. Specify the procedures that you will implement in order to reach your goals.

Step 5: Develop alternatives. Plan for more than one way to obtain your goals. (Often known as contingency planning.)

Step 6: Review and monitor your progress. Ensure that the things you do each day will bring you closer to your personal goals, even if circumstances change.

Step 7: Communicate your plan. Share your plan with some important people in your life.

In many ways you will find that personal planning is easier than planning at your job because it does not involve large groups of people. It may involve only you, or you and your spouse, or it may also involve your children and your employer. In any case, you need not be concerned with the judgments and opinions of many people. So follow the steps outlined and judge for yourself the need for personal planning.

Step 1: Know Thyself

Planning for your personal life works best if you begin by determining some important information about you and your family. After all, who knows you better than you? You might be tempted at this point to ignore Step 1; you may even tell yourself that you already know exactly what you value, so why bother? If you

(text continues on p. 74)

Values Clarification Exercise

Each of us—male or female, married or single, employer or employee—needs occasionally to be reminded of our natural tendency to behave and think in ways shaped by our definition of what our roles should be. If we are to make intelligent decisions about what is important to us in our work and family lives, we need first to sort out what we really believe (versus what we *say* we believe) about our roles and responsibilities.

This exercise is *not* a test. No score is compiled and subsequently used to assign a "best," "good," or "poor" classification. The sole purpose of the exercise is to allow you to reexamine what you *actually* believe or do, as distinct from what you like to *think* you believe or do. Answer each question honestly and instinctively; don't shy away from your feelings with excuses like "I can't answer that in the abstract; it all depends on the circumstances."

You may wish to use this exercise as a means of clarifying *your* work and family values; or you and your partner may find the results enlightening in your attempts to understand more clearly what *the other* values. Either way, much can be derived from closely comparing your beliefs and your actual behavior. At the very least, this exercise can stimulate you (and others) to question and rethink important work/family issues.

1. If your partner were offered a better job in another city, how likely is it that you would move, even though you might initially be underemployed or unemployed?

a) Very unlikely	c) Fairly likely
b) Fairly unlikely	d) Very likely

2. All in all, whose career is given more weight when you make decisions that affect both careers?

a) Yours	c) Equal weight
b) Your partner's	

3. Division of housework should be done according to individual skills and strengths; the one who does it best should do it.

   a) Agree
   b) Disagree

4. The person who makes the most money should be the major decision maker about how the money will be spent.

   a) Agree
   b) Disagree

5. If you could take a child-care leave from work after the birth of your child, would you take it?

   a) Certainly   c) Probably not
   b) Probably   d) Certainly not

6. Couples where neither partner is willing to stay at home and raise the children should not become parents.

   a) Agree
   b) Disagree

7. The more active a role in parenting a father assumes, the less likely he is to rise to the top of his profession.

   a) Agree
   b) Disagree

8. The amount of time a parent spends with a child is less important than the quality of that time.

   a) Agree
   b) Disagree

9. Having a mother who works is bad for children under six.

   a) Agree
   b) Disagree

10. Finding and selecting child care should be the responsibility of both parents.

    a) Agree
    b) Disagree

feel this way, write down as many items as you can about what you value for yourself and your family, and then test the items against your success at accomplishing those things that are *really* important to you.

A word of caution: If you are part of a dual-career family team, it is important that each partner begin by separately clarifying his or her personal values. Next the partners should share the information with each other.

An enlightening exercise is to circle all the items on your list that have little to do with money or time. You may be surprised at the number and kinds of things that you value.

Identifying and clarifying your values helps you take stock of the things that are most important to you. What is really important should serve as the basis for all the major life choices you make, such as the career you aspire to and how you rear your children. Your personal values even influence relatively minor decisions, such as vacations and clothes.

Remember, values are *not* opinions or absolutes. They are what *you* prefer based on your past and present experiences and your familial, societal, and cultural conditioning. The accompanying values clarification exercise is a good way to start. Some additional considerations for generating a personal list of values may include:

- What is essential in your life? Think of your health, relationships, work, home, and financial needs.
- Who are the important people in your life? Include spouses, children, parents, friends—and don't forget *you*.
- What do you believe about children and how they develop? What is best for *your* children?
- What do you believe your children need?
- What lifestyle do you envision for yourself and your family?
- What do you need to feel really good about yourself?
- What do you want to achieve in the next year, three years, five years?
- What constitutes a good family life?

- What constitutes a good parent?
- What constitutes a good spouse?

You will note that most of these questions deal with what *you* want for *you* and *your* family. That's not unreasonable since it is *your* life.

If you begin the planning process without an assessment of your values, you may find yourself planning for something that is totally unrealistic for you at this point in time, or something that wouldn't satisfy you even if you achieved it. As Socrates said centuries ago, "Man, know thyself."

Step 2: Assess the Situation

You need to decide where you are now in your job and in your personal life. You also need to know what external and internal factors are or will be affecting your life, such as a forthcoming promotion, baby, or a new house. Finally, it is necessary to determine your strengths and weaknesses. This exercise set the stage for determining your goals.

Step 3: Establish Your Personal Goals

Goals have been referred to as the keys to success, but what are they? People may define goals in a number of ways, or even use the term interchangeably with objectives, but almost all would agree that goals are statements of what you want for the future. Goals are usually measurable and denote end results rather than the actions taken to accomplish them. Goals must be clearly established before you can set your action plan into motion.

People should have *long-range goals* was well as *short-range goals*. Long-range goals usually reflect a desired outcome over a long period of time, while short-range goals reflect a desired outcome that is more immediate. Your short-range goals should be consistent with your long-range goals.

Remember Jean Sparkin's daily calendar of events discussed earlier in this chapter? Remember how we said that the same schedule could help Jean in planning if she used it as a tool? Currently Jean is a slave to carrying out her numerous tasks, but she is never sure which tasks are important to her value system, which need to be completed by a specific point in time, and which she could eliminate because they are not really helping her achieve her desired goals.

Jean really needs to clarify her goals. She needs to define what is vital to her personal value system, and then she needs to proceed to take *action* in order to accomplish the variety of tasks that will help her reach her goals. Knowing that the activities she engages in each day are bringing her to a desired outcome can free Jean's thinking and make sense of a harried life.

Goals can increase your ability to recognize where you are heading and help you avoid premature decision making (otherwise known as "jumping the gun").

As one family stated:

> We're the kind of people—we get frustrated so easily, we don't plan, we don't define our goals. We end up making choices and decisions before we really know what we want. We don't interview a number of caregivers just to find the one best one. Then are we sorry.

Your objective for setting goals should be to define where you want to be. If you prefer to drift aimlessly through the work/family maze, then don't plan, don't establish personal goals, and don't develop an action plan

Step 4: Put an Action Plan into Motion

Here is the point at which you take constructive action by developing step-by-step strategies and activities that are realistic, concrete, attainable, and measurable. It is important that you attach a time frame to your action steps so that you will know how much time will be devoted to a particular task, and when you may look forward to progress. In other words, stating your

(text continues on p. 80)

Personal Plan of Action Worksheet

I. Area for Consideration (e.g. child care, relocation):

_____

II. Goal (I want to achieve the following:)

_____

_____

III. Target Completion Date for Reaching This Goal: _____

IV. Action Steps Necessary to Reach This Goal (include as many as you feel are necessary):

Action Steps	*Beginning Target Date*	*Date Actually Completed*
1. _____	_____	_____
_____		
_____		
2. _____	_____	_____
_____		
_____		
3. _____	_____	_____
_____		
_____		

| | *Beginning* | *Date Actually* |
| *Action Steps* | *Target Date* | *Completed* |

4. _____   _____   _____

   _____

   _____

5. _____   _____   _____

   _____

   _____

V. *Reviewing and Monitoring Progress*

You need to decide how often you will monitor your progress. Some goals require daily monitoring, while others may require a weekly or monthly review.

1. Will I reach my goal by my beginning target date? _____

2. If not, what may be hindering me?

    Need more ability in _____ .

    Need more knowledge of _____ .

    Goal is not consistent with my overall plan. _____

    Fear of success or failure in _____ .

    Goal is more difficult than I foresaw because _____ .

    Goal is unrealistic in light of my current work/family commitments. _____

    Goal is achievable, but original target date was unrealistic.
    _____

    Other: _____

    _____

3. Do I want to continue to reach this goal? _____

4. Do I need or want to revise my goal? _____

5. If so, rewrite goal, action steps, and target dates on another page.

VI. *Evaluation*

    I know I achieved my goals when:

        1.

        2.

        3.

        4.

        5.

The most important lessons learned from this activity were:

        1.

        2.

        3.

        4.

        5.

goal and then wishing won't make your goal come true. That only happens in the movies.

The accompanying personal plan of action worksheet provides a helpful format for clarifying personal goals, developing action steps, and monitoring your progress. Feel free to adapt or duplicate the form for use with each goal; this record of information is useful for future planning.

Step 5: Develop Alternatives

You should now go back to your list of goals and determine those that are most important to your family at this point in time. Perhaps a trip to Scandinavia is not really an immediate goal in light of reduced interest rates that can make your dream house a reality now rather than three years from now. Also, you need to be sensitive to special circumstances that cause a temporary change in priorities. If things at work are running smoothly, perhaps more energy can be directed to family activities. There are times when the family faces a crisis and the balance of activities shifts to provide for this need. In other words, action steps may require flexibility and provisions for alternate plans. The important question is whether you are guiding your actions. If you are, you will be sure that your ultimate goals will be achieved.

Obviously, not every alternative can be foreseen in advance, nor can every alternative you foresee be given detailed attention. There are limitations on information, resources, and finances, but considering too many alternatives is always better than failing to recognize a really important option.

One of the strategies made clear to us by a parent we met with was the if-then technique. The father, a mathematician, used the principle of algorithms, which is a mathematical term used for a series of questions and answers, each answer indicating the next question.

> *If* I choose this schedule *then* my wife can have time to finish her schooling and maintain her job. *If* I choose another schedule *then* perhaps we do need an in-home caregiver.

This father systematically explored all possibilities to make sure he and his wife would reach their goals.

Step 6: Review and Monitor Your Progress

Making a plan and putting it in a desk drawer is not the answer to successful personal planning. You are then leaving the outcomes to chance rather than taking control over your life. Instead, it is important to review and monitor your plan as you go along to be sure it is working, and to adjust it if necessary. Remember Murphy's Laws and keep this in mind when engaging in the planning process:

1. Nothing is as simple as it seems.
2. Many things take longer than you think.
3. Anything that can go wrong will go wrong—and at the worst possible time.

Keeping these principles in mind, you can see how critical it is to review your progress in time to take corrective action. For example, your original action steps may not yield the desired results, so that new ones will have to be added. Or perhaps your original time frame was over optimistic.

It's easy to get upset, frustrated, and anxious when life does not work out as you expect it to. We can't avoid reality—things do go wrong—but detecting the problem early and responding when you have ample time is a lot less stressful than waiting until your whole plan falls apart. It's also important to remember that your plan is not a failure just because it needs adjustments for things you could not foresee in advance.

Monitoring your plan also lets you know things are going well. One parent we spoke with was so accustomed to crises that she actually felt uncomfortable when things were going right! If you prefer the excitement of teetering on the edge of disaster, then don't review your plans.

Step 7: Communicate Your Plan

Because your work and family life involve dynamic social systems, it is important that you communicate effectively your goals to employers, spouse, friends, child-care workers, pediatricians, business associates, or anyone else affected by them. In fact, if you can't communicate your objectives, go back and rethink what you really believe, what you really want, and where you want to be heading during the next six months or year. You may not always choose to share your personal goals with everyone, but you can't expect people to cooperate with you unless they really know what you want.

Unless you communicate your goals and the action you will take toward meeting them, many people will make assumptions about your plans—assumptions that may be incorrect. The employer who gives all your unfinished projects to someone else probably does not know that you *plan* to keep up with your job at home during your child-care leave—or may not even feel sure that you will return to your job at all.

An Example of the Personal Planning Process

To help you visualize the personal planning process more clearly, here's an example of the process at work in a situation many working parents are familiar with. This imaginary scene presents a set of circumstances that may prompt different responses and behaviors from different people. What is important to remember here is that the form *your* planning takes depends on *you.*

Joan Kirk is an executive of a major corporation and is expecting her first child in a few short months. She has been successful in her work and is determined to be successful as a parent—to rear a loving, independent, happy, competent child. Joan knows, too, that work is an important part of her life. Where does Joan go from here, given her circumstances?

Step 1: Know Thyself

Joan begins by *acknowledging some personal values*. She writes this list:

- I believe that integrating work and family is necessary for the well-being of my family.
- I believe in attempting to balance time between people I love and my work.
- I believe work is an integral part of my life, and that excellence at work is essential.
- I believe that affordable, reliable, quality child-care arrangements will soon be necessary to meet my family's needs.
- I believe that the first three months of a child's life are especially important to the development of the child.
- I believe child care should begin at three months.
- I believe that keeping up with the latest developments in my profession is crucial.

Joan discusses her list with her husband, Tim, and they find that most of their value statements are compatible. Tim has mixed feelings at first about Joan returning to work so soon, but given her situation at work he agrees that a three-month maternity leave is the best option.

Step 2: Assess the Situation

After evaluating her situation at work and at home, Joan needs to review her list of value statements to determine what are the most important considerations on the list. Two obviously important goals are to arrange a maternity leave and to find suitable child care. Joan needs to work toward concentrating on these goals first. Does this mean Joan has no other goals? Certainly not; it only means that in the current situation, these are her first two priorities. (For this example, we'll focus on finding child care.)

Step 3: Establish Your Personal Goals

Joan and Tim decide that their *immediate* (short-range) goal is:

> To educate ourselves about child care during the next few weeks.

Their *long-range goal* is:

> To identify and make all necessary arrangements for suitable, quality child care by the time the baby is two months old.

Now Joan and Tim can put the plan into motion. They can decide on the steps they need to take to reach the goal of finding suitable quality child care.

Step 4: Put an Action Plan into Motion

Joan comes up with these action steps to meet her goal:

- I will research child-care options in the library by _____.
- I will visit a minimum of five child-care settings by _____.
- Tim will talk with at least three working parents about their child-care arrangements by _____.
- Tim will check with the child-care agencies in our community by _____. (See Appendix E for listing of resources on this topic.)
- We will develop a personal checklist for child care that agrees with our child's needs, my personal needs, and Tim's needs by _____.

- We will make a decision about child-care arrangements by _____.

Note the number of steps necessary to fulfill the one goal of finding quality child care, and the time frame that will be needed for each step.

Step 5: Develop Alternatives

In the course of discussing the need for quality child care with friends and colleagues, Joan and Tim are told about an organization that helps to identify and train young women who want to be nannies. Although Joan had not planned to hire an in-home caregiver for her baby, she recognizes that a nanny should be considered. Joan and Tim also recognize that a nanny would allow Joan some free time which she could use to continue to keep up with her professional interests during Joan's three-month maternity leave.

Step 6: Review and Monitor Your Plan

After two weeks of visiting selected child care centers, Joan and Tim find that the centers have inadequate infant programs which will not meet the child care needs they have outlined. They recognize that visiting five child care centers is insufficient and that their plan needs revision. Joan and Tim plan to visit an additional five to ten child care centers. Joan and Tim recognize that they need to learn more about the infant-toddler curriculum. They plan to contact the Department of Early Childhood Education at a local college to get more information about quality programs for infants. Tim convinces Joan to register with the organization that recruits and trains nannies. Although Joan and Tim's plan required changes, it was not nearly as frustrating as being without any options. They continue to work toward identified goals that take into account their essential needs as individuals and as a family.

Step 7: Communicate Your Plan

Joan arranges to meet with her employer to discuss her career path for the next six months to one year and work out the details of her maternity leave.

In their meeting, Joan and her employer outline a timetable and guidelines for Joan's maternity leave. Joan feels strongly that her three month maternity leave should provide her with uninterrupted time with her child. However, she does agree to respond to written memos from her employer to ensure that Joan will keep up with what is happening at the office. As a member of a management team, Joan also agrees to finish all pending projects before her maternity leave. Her employer agrees that no new projects will be given to Joan for at least four weeks before her departure. Joan and her employer are satisfied, and both agree to abide by the terms of the arrangement. Communicating her plan has not only helped Joan and Tim, but her colleagues as well. And the baby will benefit, too.

Is this example meant to portray an ideal situation or the one right way? Certainly not. The example of Joan and Tim is meant to remind you that planning offers you freedom. You need not be a slave to the urgency day-to-day living. You can know that you control your personal life. Victor Hugo said, ''Where no plan is laid, where the disposal of time is surrendered merely to chance, chaos soon reigns.''

What to Do When You're Up to Your Ears in Alligators

There's a humorous saying, ''When you're up to your ears in alligators, who cares about the plan for clearing the swamp?'' Perhaps that is how you feel right now about personal planning: You're too busy with crises to have time to plan.

The trouble is, the less you plan, the more alligators you'll run into! Many parents risk the ease, flexibility, spontaneity, and freedom they long for by not taking the time now to develop personal plans that can in fact make their lives simpler and more manageable. Creating a plan that is consistent with your values gives you the pleasant feeling of being in control a good deal of the time. It also diminishes the need to battle alligators at every turn and enhances your perception of yourself as a competent person.

We recognize that the work/family journey is not an easy one. Most families meet with detours—sometimes through swamps!—and a crisis may prevent them from staying with a well-planned journey. This makes them feel confused, frustrated, and stressed.

If you are comfortable with the personal planning process, you may be able to readily note the detours in the road when you are confronted by them, and adapt your plan to overcome the new forks in the road. The best plans may need to be revised and reworked. Sometimes it is necessary, as Robert Frost said, to take a road "less traveled by" in order to reach the goals that make a difference for you. Revising your plan is often a means of identifying all your alternatives so that you can choose those most helpful to you.

The pressures of attempting to balance work and family make us all feel overburdened some of the time. We all know about the stumbling blocks, the daily crises, the problems at home and at our jobs, the hurried decision making, and the need for fire fighting, but we urge you not to avoid personal planning. Instead, consider the rewards of knowing the path *you* personally want to take in merging your work and family lives. Time spent on planning is worth it!

Roadblock No. 4: The Dragnet School of Problem Solving

A problem well defined is half solved.

—John Dewey
Democracy and Education

For years, Detectives Friday and Gannon from the popular television series *Dragnet* showed America how to solve a problem. Week after week, Friday and Gannon were called upon by their boss to investigate some civil or criminal conflict. Week after week, the two stared solemnly at each other and gravely went into the streets of Los Angeles to begin their sleuthing. The detectives traveled door to door, talking with anyone who might be able to tell them how the problem started, who was involved, what happened. Often Detectives Friday and Gannon would have to caution the people they spoke with: no subjective impressions, no conjectures, "just the facts, please." The policemen never forgot the first lesson they learned in the Dragnet School of Problem Solving: Find the facts and you'll find the problem. Find the problem and you'll find the solution.

Where We Go Wrong: Dossiers of Accusations

Joan Hirsch and Doug Adams are staunch advocates of the Dragnet Method. They consider themselves fact finders of the highest order. When faced with conflict, they turn into bustling detectives, hot on the trail of facts that will lead them to The Problem. They postpone discussion and exchange of theories until their separate investigations are complete. Then, armed with bulging dossiers of facts, they release their findings in a joint accusation exercise, one of many games working parents play.

Joan begins, clearing her throat. "The Problem," she announced solemnly, "can be summed up in two words: Unhelpful Doug." Noting her husband's annoyed expression, she blurts out a series of facts that support her conclusion:

Fact 1. Unhelpful Doug doesn't pick up his clothes.

Fact 2. Despite several requests, Unhelpful Doug doesn't clean up the bathroom.

Fact 3. Joan has to take time out of her busy schedule every week to go grocery shopping, a task repugnant to Unhelpful Doug.

Fact 4. Responsibility for getting their daughter Sara dressed and fed in the morning remains exclusively Joan's.

Fact 5 is drowned out as Doug decides he's heard enough and begins to recite the results of his own investigation.

"Joan," Doug says patiently, "I'm afraid your memory is getting worse." Stories of barbecued dinners, folded laundry, and the car being warmed up on cold winter mornings follow. More facts could be noted, Doug asserts, but clearly Joan begins to see that the label of Unhelpful Doug is unwarranted.

Sensing he's on a roll, Doug forges ahead and boldly declares his view of The Problem: "Demanding Joan." And is she ever demanding! She constantly talks during Dan Rather (Fact 1), insists that Doug do household chores that she will redo later when she discovers he didn't do them right (Fact 2), and is irritated when Doug falls asleep at the dinner table after a night on call at the hospital (Fact 3).

Something has backfired. The method Joan and Doug thought would lead to a solution pushes them further away from a solution and each other. In the process, resentments are reinforced, feelings are bruised, and anger is stimulated. The Problem defies their efforts to define it and a truce is declared. Vague promises of trying harder are exchanged. Conflict continues.

When juggling the conflicting demands of home and work, it is easy to lapse into certain destructive behavioral patterns. These patterns may help us in the short run to attain a sense of control, but they sow the seeds for resentment and even greater conflict in the future.

As with all habits, it's hard to see them until they're pointed out to us. Take some time with your family to read through the accompanying description of ten games working parents play.

Ask others whether they see you engaging in certain behavioral games, and identify which ones you see yourself or others playing. Talk about the reasons why you (or they) might slip into such habits, and what you can do to break out of them.

Contrast Joan and Doug's experiences with those of Diane Robbins, a 38-year-old international marketing specialist, and her husband Kevin, a science teacher in the public schools. The two acknowledged a more-than-passing acquaintance with conflict. Despite their struggles, Diane laughingly claimed, "But I really do get everything I want!"

In response to the skeptical look on our faces, she added:

> I know that I've sacrificed and I know I'm not spoiled. It's just that I want what I know can work out. I don't ask for the world; I ask for what's possible and conceivable. I don't expect great, unreachable things . . . it makes sense what I want.

Diane and Kevin both see themselves as winners. Kevin hasn't found the satisfaction he needs in his job, yet remains optimistic. Diane is, as she says, his "ticket": her earning power will enable

Ten Games Working Parents Play

Game	Behavior
1. The schedule slave	"Look, I really don't have time for that; I understand it's important to you, but my schedule is really tight this week."
2. The efficiency expert	"No, I'm listening. I just always do two or three things at the same time!"
3. The tune-out artist	"What did you say? I was thinking about what I've got to do later."
4. The forgetter	"I know I was supposed to pick up the dry cleaning, but you know me—I never remember details like that!"
5. The escape artist	"Look, I'll be in my study tonight working. Call me if you really need something."
6. The martyr	"Oh, don't worry about me. You go ahead and get what you need; I'll manage."
7. The office blamer	"I wanted to be able to spend time with you this weekend, but you know how the boss is."
8. The helpless creature	"I would help out more around the house, but I don't know how to do a lot of things."
9. The truly competent parent	"Don't pick her up like that, you should—Oh, never mind, just give her to me."
10. Superparent	"No problem. I'm used to juggling a lot of things at one time."

him to look around, survey his options, and feel comfortable with the idea of a midcareer change.

Is it possible to confront conflict head-on and have both parties emerge winners? Diane and Kevin, and many of the other parents we spoke with, say it is. They have rejected the win-or-lose strategy as ineffective and replaced it with an alternative approach: negotiation.

What Every Negotiator Needs to Know

Negotiation conjures up images of smoke-filled rooms and tense, hostile exchanges; Henry Kissinger and Shuttle Diplomacy; Day 31 of the Hostage Crisis. Most of us treat negotiation as a process where we draw up a list of demands, second-guess our opponents, and call each other's bluff. After all, isn't negotiation just a nice name for a cold and calculating game in which each player tries to get the most while giving up the least?

Not really. We're all negotiators. As kids, we negotiated with other kids. (''I'm sick of this game. How about trading it for your bike?'') As neophytes, we sometimes made outrageous offers. If we did, we could count on being told as much as our playmates snatched up their possessions indignantly and went home. And of course we negotiated with our parents, just as our children negotiate with us and we with them. (''You can stay up tonight if you're good.'' ''If I finish all my macaroni, can I go over to Marlene's after dinner?'') The list of our experiences with negotiation is endless: as students, with teachers; as husbands, with wives; as lawyers, with lawyers; as shoppers, with car salesmen; as employers, with employees.

With all our experience as negotiators, you'd think we would be experts by now. But negotiation is like math: Just because we've been learning and using the subject matter for a long time doesn't mean we're proficient. How good we are at math or negotiation depends on how well we grasped the basics. Unlike math students, most of us have not had teachers to help us acquire negotiation skills. It's been strictly trial and error, and as a result, we often think we're negotiating when we're not. Few of us could say what the process involves, and even fewer could pinpoint what we need to do to improve.

It's Not *Let's Make a Deal*

Contrary to popular belief, negotiation is nothing like the television game show *Let's Make a Deal*. Game shows in general are based on a win-or-lose approach. Contestants are pitted against one another in a clash of irreconcilable interests. All participants want to win; only one can. Each player must push the button, guess the answer, pick the right door, or choose the correct card *before* his or her opponent does.

A negotiator views conflict much the way a piano tuner sees an out-of-tune piano. Both perceive a state of disharmony which, with skillful adjustments and intervention, can be corrected. Consequently, negotiators don't perceive conflict as something to avoid. Instead, they see it as an opportunity to engage in negotiation, *the process in which we search for ways to satisfy opposing needs through creating and implementing a range of solutions.* Through negotiation, we can tap our creativity and release our emotions. We are forced to confront ourselves and to examine our motivations, our fears, our assumptions, and our hopes. We gain a better understanding of the needs of others and an enhanced awareness of their humanity.

Identifying Shared Interests and Capitalizing on Differences

A negotiator sees the potential in conflict, not the destruction. But negotiation is more than a positive mental state. It's a process, a method of conflict resolution and problem solving that often begins with the parties identifying their shared interests and capitalizing on their differences.

Take, for example, Mark and Carla Pierson, whom you met

in Chapter 3, as they describe the solution they found to the dilemma "Who'll Do What in the Kitchen?"

> We each do different things well. She does the dishes and I cook the meals. The reason I cook the meals is I *hate* doing the dishes. And in order to get what I want—it's my token. It's tokenism, okay? I give her the token of making dinner and she gives me the token of washing dishes.

In Mark and Carla's case, their shared interests are many: They would like meal preparation and clean-up to proceed as smoothly as possible, with minimal cost to each person's mental and physical state; they want to be fair; and they want to preserve their relationship. Carla is indifferent about cooking and doing the dishes; Mark despises the latter. Guided by their shared interests, they look to their differences to provide a basis for resolving their conflicts.

Disagreement, differences, opposing interests—we tend to see these as the root of our problems. Ironically enough, they can be used as the framework for our agreements. Remember the old nursery rhyme about the Sprats?

> Jack Sprat could eat no fat,
> His wife could eat no lean,
> And so betwixt them both, you see,
> They licked the platter clean.

Their differences, whether natural or developed, were their salvation.

In the midst of a conflict, most of us have no trouble identifying our differences. Recognizing our shared interests presents more of a problem, but it is essential to the negotiation process. We should ask ourselves: What do we have at stake here? What are the costs we'll bear if we don't resolve this issue? What benefits will we enjoy if we can reach agreement? Identification of common interests not only reminds us why we are even attempting to find a solution to our differences, but can help diffuse the powerful emotions that often accompany conflict.

The skilled negotiator understands that a solution must satisfy the needs of those involved. He or she recognizes that identifying shared interests and differences is crucial to formulating viable options.

Needs: The Powerful Motivators

When negotiators shift their focus in problem solving from fact finding to need finding, they are in some ways exchanging a micro lens for a macro lens. After all, they are negotiating, not reporting. A negotiator's task isn't to unearth the who, what, when, where, and how; his or her real concern is *why*. Why would (or wouldn't) your employer be inclined to work out a child-care leave with you? Why are you irritated with the child-care center? Why is Joan angry when Doug wants to watch the nightly news without interruptions? Why does it bother you so much that your son seems to enjoy being with his mother more than with you?

The question "Why?" rarely has but one answer. Our behavior is generally motivated by a combination of needs, not just one. Doug's passion for Dan Rather may be a response to his need to be alone for a while after his return from work; it may satisfy his need to feel competent and well informed; perhaps it is Doug's way of maintaining a link with the outside world while in a career that threatens to engulf him with its demands. More than likely, his behavior has nothing to do with Joan's interpretation, "My husband enjoys Dan Rather's company more than mine."

At the root of our conflicts with our employers and our children, our child's caregivers, our spouses and ex-spouses, are *unsatisfied needs*. These are the true basis for negotiation. If we can identify and communicate our needs to others and understand the reasons for their behavior, then we can look for appropriate solutions.

Defining Our Needs

How do we go about defining our unsatisfied needs? Aren't they obvious, both to us and the people we deal with? The answer to the second question is a resounding "No!" Our *positions* may be obvious ("I don't want to cook dinner tonight," "I can't pick up Carl from the sitter's," "We can't give you a paid child-care leave"). But after all, our positions are versions of our needs, edited and altered for social acceptability. This is true especially in transitional times, when our needs are based on our current situation and emotions but our positions reflect past definitions of acceptable behavior.

Probably the best place to start in the need-finding process is to recognize and examine our feelings in the problem situation. Do I feel angry, hurt, challenged, fearful, insecure? Focusing on emotional and physical reactions can provide valuable insight into defining which of our needs are not being met.

To illustrate the discrepancy between positions and needs, let's return to Joan and Doug. One of their points of contention centers around Doug's desire to watch the evening news without interruption. Joan's position is "I don't mind you watching the news when you get home, but I end up making dinner by myself while you just sit around." Doug's position is defensive: "I enjoy watching the news, and my hours as a resident don't leave me much time to do the little things I like." Both positions contain a kernel of truth, but present a distorted image of Joan's and Doug's needs.

Joan's feelings are a collage of resentment, hurt, and anger. She resents Doug for not realizing that she also would like to sit down and watch the news. She is hurt that in the little time they can spend together, Doug would prefer to spend that first half-hour at home watching television. And Joan is angry that Doug doesn't offer to make dinner and take care of their child so she too can relax.

Doug also feels resentment, hurt, and anger, but for different reasons. He resents Joan for denying him one of his few remaining pleasures. He is hurt that Joan seems oblivious to the strain and pressures he lives under at work, and he is angry that she isn't like his mother, who he is sure never refused such a small favor to his father.

Once Joan and Doug have recognized their feelings, they can start to expose some of the unsatisfied needs that are embedded within their positions. Joan may find that she needs to feel needed and derives some positive reinforcement from the act of "selflessly" preparing dinner and taking care of Sara while her husband relaxes. Doug could discover that his need to be admired isn't being met by Joan and he uses the half-hour of forced noncommunication to punish her. In the process of examining their positions, the couple may learn some things about themselves that contradict the images they present to the public and to each other. Acknowledging and confronting these conflicts is hard, but unless Doug and Joan identify and accept their needs, their negotiations will be futile.

Putting the Pieces Together: Communicating to Resolve Conflict

Finding needs presents an opportunity to learn more about ourselves and each other, but it won't help resolve a conflict unless we communicate those needs. Just as with personal planning, when we communicate our needs to our children, our employer, or any other person, we are placing our pieces of the jigsaw puzzle on the table. Those pieces represent our perceptions of a conflict and our goals. The remaining pieces emerge when the other party expresses his other needs to us. The subject of negotiations—the basis of our conflict—is identified mutually through an exchange of definitions based on each person's needs.

How well we put the pieces of the puzzle together depends on how effectively we communicate our needs. If we miscommunicate, we run the risk of losing or misplacing a crucial piece of the puzzle. Our chances of success in negotiation are greater when we:

1. Decide to address one source of conflict at a time.
2. Select issues that are present- and future-oriented, not grievances of the past.
3. Define our needs clearly and specifically.
4. Take the other party's needs as seriously as we take our own.

When Items 1 and 2 were mentioned to one of the families we interviewed, the husband laughed and nodded approvingly. "That's one of my weak spots," he acknowledged. "Bobbie and I start out talking about one thing and before I know it, I start bringing up everything that's been bugging me for the past six months—sometimes, six years!"

Many communication experts advise adopting a statute of limitations on "past crimes." Such a cut-off date discourages us from dragging out dirty laundry every few months, and essentially forces us to wash it or put it away. Tackling one problem at a time helps avoid spreading our energies too thin. When we focus on a specific need that remains unmet, the probability of figuring out a way to satisfy that need is greater. Simultaneous examination of all unsatisfied needs can be overwhelming.

All of us have a tendency to communicate in vague terms when we feel unsure or embarrassed, or are simply trying to avoid something. Statements like "I need more help" or "I just want to be alone" are blurred snapshots of our needs. They give a rough idea of the boundaries or form, but lack the detail viewers need to recognize what they're looking at. Hard though it is, we should strive to articulate our needs in clear, specific terms. Only then can we expect another person to understand what it is that we're looking for and really want.

Item 4 involves more than the familiar old saying "Put yourself in his shoes." It's not enough to intellectually comprehend the other person's point of view; we have to *feel* it. We have to understand it with the same intensity that we understand our own needs. We have to see the ins and outs of it. We have to experience true empathy. The ability to transcend oneself and feel another's emotions is the most challenging and valuable trait a negotiator can develop. Without it, the jigsaw puzzle will always be a little off-center, and some pieces won't quite fit.

It's not uncommon for people to conclude the solution-searching phases of their negotiations with comments like:

- What I need just doesn't exist!
- We've come up with all these great solutions, but there's one small hitch: They either cost too much or they're not available in our community.

When sentiments such as these are voiced, they're not a sign of failed negotiations. Rather, they signal the need to move to a new stage in the negotiation process in which we *reevaluate assumptions* and possibly *create new options*.

Testing Our Assumptions

Assumptions in and of themselves aren't bad. But when we begin to treat them as facts we run into trouble. Assumptions disguised as facts have the converse effect of optical illusions. Illusions convince us something's there when it's not; many common assumptions convince us nothing's there when something is.

Assumptions cloaked as facts reveal themselves when parents ruefully remark:

- I'd love to have that kind of child care, but it's too expensive.
- There's no way that my boss would consider a job-sharing arrangement.
- I never have any time for myself, but that's just the way things are.
- If things are going to get done around this office, I've got to do them myself.

- Our son is having a lot of problems and we're sure it's because we don't spend enough time with him.

Maybe they're right. Maybe the boss won't consider a job-sharing arrangement. Maybe the kind of child care they'd love to have is too expensive. If so, they must begin to explore new options, ones that don't exist.

On the other hand, maybe they're wrong. Maybe their facts are really assumptions based on false perceptions.

Consider for a moment the story of the sisters who were quarreling bitterly over who would use the last orange in the refrigerator. Both girls had been invited to a party that night; both were planning a surprise dish for their friends. Both of their recipes called for an orange, and no more oranges could be found since the grocery stores had closed for the evening. In frustration, one sister finally grabbed the orange in dispute and tossed it in the garbage, declaring, "This is ridiculous! If you get the orange, I'll be angry, and vice versa! Either way, one of us loses." Only later did it surface that one sister had wanted the fruit of the orange (minus the peel) for her recipe, while the other wanted the peel (minus the fruit) for hers. They had seen one solution only, a solution built on false assumptions, and it cost them a much better solution to their dispute.

We make hundreds, even thousands, of assumptions about the way our lives are, how they must be, how many choices we really have, how other people feel about our choices, and how we implement them. It would be impossible to validate every assumption we make. But when we've reached a certain point in negotiating with our spouse or our boss or our kids or even ourselves and we keep spinning our wheels, reevaluating our assumptions about the issue at hand may pull us out of the mud.

How do we find out whether our assumptions are on target? One way is to educate ourselves. We do it every time we read a restaurant review or an issue of *Consumer Reports*; why not take the time to do it about the deeper issues that really interfere with the balance of work and family? Find out whether that kind of child care you want is as expensive as you think it is. More importantly, find out whether it's really the appropriate situation for your shy three-year-old. Contact organizations that can give you information on how to set up a joint custody agreement. Stop assuming that there is one best family form that meets the needs of children. *Question your assumptions.* As Suzanne La-Follette remarked in 1926, "There is nothing more innately human than the tendency to transmute what has become customary into what has been divinely ordained."[18]

The risks of blindly following our assumptions are great. We can find ourselves:

- Doing more than we have to, because we assume that it must be done or that no one else can or will help us.
- Doing less than we can, because we assume that it's impossible to do more of what we want.
- Berating ourselves about what we're doing, because we ignore the inner assumptions that clash with our professed beliefs.

Should we discover that our assumptions are correct—that the boss is unfavorably disposed toward anything less than a full-time work schedule, or that the child care we want is just as expensive as we thought—we need to take a deep breath and inflate our options balloon. Most of the time, we treat our choices as though they were one-dimensional, like a deflated balloon lying flat on the surface of a table. We rank our choices along a continuum, from "most favorable for her or them" to "most favorable for me."

It is perhaps in this area—creating new choices that don't appear on the balloon's surface but rather emerge as it is inflated—that we can learn the most from each other. Repeatedly, as we listened to parents tell us how they are handling their conflicts, we were struck by the fact that *people are never without creative alternatives, no matter what their circumstances.*

The very fact that such a claim will be read with disbelief is more a reflection of our own biases—our own roadblocks that obscure the range of choices we can have—than a reflection of the improbability of the statement.

In the next chapter we will look at the ways in which parents are inflating their balloon of choices.

5

Inflating Your Options Balloon

No one is without creative alternatives, no matter what his circumstances.

—Gerald I. Nierenberg
The Art of Creative Thinking

In Chapter 4 we discussed some of the challenges most often encountered by working parents, challenges that can deflate their balloon of choices and change its form from multidimensional to one-dimensional. Too many working parents treat their deflated balloon as though it were constructed of cement rather than rubber. We hope the creative strategies that follow will help you inflate your options balloon. These strategies, utilized by the working parents we met with, helped them overcome the challenges they faced in integrating their work and family lives, primarily through rediscovery and tapping an internal resource we have all learned to repress and undervalue over the years. This resource has often been forced to exist in hibernation, and yet research tells us that it is displayed by 90 percent of five-year-olds. By age seven, it is discernible in only 10 percent of children; evidence of its existence further shrinks to 2 percent in adulthood. The resource we speak of, so often seen in young children and so rarely in adults, is *creativity*.

Where Has Our Creativity Gone?

There are many forces that lobby against expression of our creativity; it's small wonder that we actively suppress it. Conformity is rewarded at school, at home, and at work. Active imaginations are tamed in the name of social order; logical, reasonable, rational behavior is encouraged and interpreted as a sign of maturity.

Michelle Wong, a former preschool teacher, described her firsthand experience with the negative reaction creative behavior often engenders.

> When I was a student teacher at a child-care center, I had a little boy in my class whose name was Aaron. I don't think I was in the class more than an hour before it became very apparent that Aaron was, in the teachers' eyes, a "problem child." I've always been a champion of the underdog, so that in itself was enough to immediately endear Aaron to me!
>
> During the next few weeks I spent in that classroom, my supervising teachers gave me a lot of reasons why they thought Aaron was such a problem. In my mind, many of them boiled down to the fact that he was active and imaginative, and beyond their control.
>
> Every Monday, the kids had a sort of show-and-tell, and we'd sit there and look at their dolls and cars and talking toys—the same things week after week. One day it was Aaron's turn to talk about what he'd brought, and he seemed very excited and happy. Pulling out two empty Crayola crayon boxes, he launched into a long explanation about how you could use the boxes to transform your hands from human hands into robot hands. He looked so pleased with himself and proceeded to put on and take off the boxes, showing us how easy yet miraculous the transformation was.

The teachers rolled their eyes at one another and quickly moved on to another child, telling Aaron to find the crayons he'd dumped out of the boxes and put them "back where they belonged." Over lunch, one of the other teachers told me how sad she thought it was that Aaron had to resort to such schemes to draw attention to himself. Creativity did not appear to be a top-priority item in this class.

And so the Aaron in all of us often gets crushed under the weight of verbal and nonverbal messages that convey the idea that the unexpected, the unusual, and the untraditional are not acceptable. Criticism of the novel concept is often automatic, and we hear ourselves and others saying in response to new ideal:

- That's not really feasible.
- It's a great idea, but it'll never work.
- I already tried that before and it didn't work.
- Let's not muddy the waters: We've got enough problems.
- That's okay in the ivory tower, but it's time to come back to reality.

Thawing Out Our Frozen Creativity

Alex Osborn, the originator of brainstorming as a problem-solving technique, believed that premature criticism and judgment inhibit creativity. The deliberate act of setting aside our critical faculties during the idea-generating phase of searching for solutions was, he felt, essential to achieving maximum productivity. Charles Clark concurs in *Idea Management: How to Motivate Creativity and Innovation.* He likens many of our idea-creating efforts to trying to get hot water out of a faucet while the cold water is running. "We can't get hot ideas out of people's heads," Clark cautions, "while the cold water of criticism is turned on. At best, we get lukewarm ideas."[19]

In our approach to problematic issues in work and family life, we must initially give free rein to our imagination, permitting it to flow unchecked by judgment. This is no easy task because we've been conditioned to be cautious, and to look before we leap. There *is* a time and place for our rational selves in conflict resolution, but it comes much later when we are selecting and evaluating our options.

Remember Laurie Brown, the law school student we talked about in Chapter 4, under Roadblock No. 1?

> I was convinced that no one in law school cared—about me, my kids, my family problems. At the suggestion of a friend in another city, I advertised at the university for other women in similar situations. The result was the formation of a support group that has gone on for years. It started out with three of us and changed dramatically over the years. It was extremely helpful to talk to other mothers in the same situation. It was a place where you could talk about work and kids together. We came up with all kinds of ideas for working things out—to get through school and be good Moms.

Laurie's story had a happy ending. However, witness the crippling effect of premature judgment in the case of Sherry and Alan Walker. The two are currently immersed in the classic dilemma of the dual-career couple: how to stay together when pursuit of professional and personal goals seems to be pushing them apart.

Sherry, age 30, has just started a Ph.D. program in Cincinnati. It's one of the few programs in the country offering the course of studies she's interested in, and to make things even more tantalizing, she was selected for a university fellowship. For the past few months, Sherry has felt that her life is really coming together: At long last, she remarks, she's found her niche.

Alan, on the other hand, has grown sour on Cincinnati. He feels unappreciated in his job, and increasingly has questioned the utility of the long and stressful hours he spends in his position as a hospital administrator. He sometimes wonders whether a career change is in order, but most of the time feels that a change of employer would go far toward eliminating his unhappiness. At a conference in March, he expresses his feelings to several colleagues, sending out the informal message that he is looking for a good opportunity. A few days later, Alan receives a phone call from a hospital in Florida, inviting him for an interview.

The conflict confronting Alan and Sherry comes to a head later that evening, as the two sit in front of their fireplace and discuss the day's events. After delivering a lecture familiar to many dual-career families (''How could you do this to me just when things were going so well?'') Sherry tries to approach the situation more rationally.

Sherry: Well, so what are our choices?

Alan: Well, if you really feel that you can't find anything you want outside Cincinnati, maybe we'll have to live apart until you finish school. Or—

Sherry: Commuter marriages are great for magazine articles and books, but they don't work in the real world. We might as well sign a death certificate for our marriage!

Alan: Well, I *suppose* I could stay here and look for something else in town. I don't know, it might—

Sherry: Don't be ridiculous! It's obvious you don't want to stay at the job you're at now and you know perfectly well there's nothing else here in town. I don't know why you're even bringing this up; you're not going to do it anyway.

Leaving Sherry and Alan by the fireplace, we return to our point: The time for judgment on the merits of options is *not* when you're looking for solutions but rather when you're selecting or evaluating them. In the solution-generating stage, your focus should be on production of a quantity of ideas, not necessarily on their quality. The more alternatives you come up with, the greater your chances of hitting on one or two that will pass the reality test.

Creativity is a crucial resource during the initial stage of inflating your options balloon when you are trying to churn out as many solutions as possible. How and where you unleash your creativity depends on what works for you. Some people heartily endorse the saying "Two heads are better than one." Others feel their productivity is greatest when they're working alone with pen and paper or tape recorder. Some individuals need to situate themselves in a comfortable room, with unobtrusive lighting and sounds; others actively seek out a table in a noisy restaurant; others don their headphones and close their eyes. Whatever has worked for you in the past: Use it! Whatever works for someone else: Try it!

A word of warning to those who are a little rusty in the creativity department: The image of ideas gushing forth like water released from a dam is appealing, but not likely to occur. Ideas are more likely to trickle out, perhaps with an occasional spurt. Frozen creativity is like a 25-pound turkey in the freezer. Neither will thaw on command, but both will come around, given a certain amount of time and effort. Some thawing techniques take longer than others. Some are more effective, some require outside help. But all of them can work.

The Ice Breakers

We all have problems getting started once in a while. We avoid plunging into the icy waters of problem solving, and find temporary comfort by locating the right pen or paper, straightening up the desk, sharpening all our pencils, or making last-minute phone calls. It's almost as if we think postponement of the beginning will allow us to skip that stage altogether and move right to the middle or end.

Wrong. We must start at the beginning. But how do we squeeze out those first few ideas?

Attribute Listing

One method that may be useful is called attribute listing. Described originally by Robert Crawford, the process begins by identifying all the major attributes or characteristics of the idea or problem being considered. When you've exhausted your list of characteristics, stop. Return to the beginning of your list and devise as many modifications of each attribute as you can. Remember, your evaluation/judgment switch is turned off at this point.

Using Sherry and Alan's dilemma as an example, what are some of the major attributes of their situation? A few that come to mind immediately are:

- Location of Alan's job and Sherry's program
- Duration of Alan's job and Sherry's program
- Cost of Alan's job and Sherry's program
- Content of Alan's job and Sherry's program

Stopping with these four, let's return to the first attribute—location. What are the possible variations of this factor?

Alan and Sherry, either together or individually, could work or study:

- At home
- In Cincinnati
- Within daily commuting distance of Cincinnati
- Within weekly commuting distance of Cincinnati
- Within monthly commuting distance of Cincinnati
- Together in the same geographic area
- Apart, in different geographic areas
- In the United States
- In a foreign country

The purpose of the exercise is to produce as many variations on each theme as you can. Once you've compiled a list of possibilities, you can start combining them (location variation 1 with duration possibility 3 with cost option 5, and so on).

Assumptional Analysis

A second ice breaker is a favorite of public policy analysts: assumptional analysis. Don't be put off by the name. This method is particularly appropriate when you know you've got a conflict but you and the other parties can't even agree as to what the conflict is about. Assumptional analysis is traditionally a five-stage process, but for our purposes, only the first three steps are necessary.

Step 1: Stakeholder Identification

The assumptional analysis method starts with what policy analysts refer to as stakeholder identification. Whose interests are at stake in the problem before you? How extensive is each person's involvement, in the short and long run? How much influence can, or should, each of the shareholders exert on the decision-making process? Unless you take into account *all* the parties who have a role in a conflict, you run the risk of ignoring their needs in our search for resolution.

Alan and Sherry, in the discussions described earlier, are guilty of pretending they live in a vacuum. Clearly more people than the couple alone have an interest in the type of solution reached. Alan's colleagues at work, both the people he works for and those who work under him, have an interest in what Alan decides to do. Sherry's professors and classmates similarly are affected by her presence or absence. Family, friends, landlords, planned but unborn children—all have a direct and indirect interest in what the couple elect for their future. Alan and Sherry shouldn't try to judge what kind of decision would benefit or hurt each of these parties at this stage of generating as many options as possible, but they should broaden their scope of analysis to include the needs and interests of all parties.

Step 2: Analysis of Possible Solutions

After stakeholder identification is complete, put together a list of possible solutions to the problem. Each time you think of a solution, follow it up by thinking backward to all the assumptions that would *support* that solution. For example, if Alan and Sherry decide to live apart for the duration of Sherry's Ph.D. program, one or more of the following assumptions would probably be true:

- Alan finds a good job away from Cincinnati.
- Sherry is unable to find or be admitted to a comparable Ph.D. program out of Cincinnati.
- Sherry is committed to the Cincinnati program and wouldn't transfer even if she could.
- Alan and Sherry are able to arrange a regular visitation schedule.
- Alan and Sherry are comfortable with the idea of living apart but seeing each other on weekends or monthly.
- Alan and Sherry both feel their careers come first now.
- There are no good employment opportunities in Cincinnati for Alan.
- The psychological costs of Alan's present job outweigh the benefits of living together in Cincinnati.

Step 3: Challenging Your Assumptions

After you have surfaced the assumptions each proposed solution rests on, challenge each underlying assumption by its antithesis. Instead of "Alan and Sherry both feel their careers come first now," ask whether the opposite ("Alan and Sherry don't feel their careers come first now") is more truthful. Scrutinizing each assumption by challenging it with a counterassumption helps you zero in on your real interests.

Anne Ferguson, an executive for a *Fortune* 500 company, demonstrates this point in the following comment:

> My assumption always was, "100 percent commitment to my job is crucial." During the first eight weeks of my child's

life I made it clear that anytime people needed anything, they could call me. I even offered to come into my office for a few hours. Suddenly (or at some point) I said to myself, "Is this really necessary? I need to consider the effects of my behavior on myself, my child, my spouse, my employer." So my commitment is still there, but there is something else. I have more balance now, because others are affected by my decisions. I now have another big responsibility, every bit as big as my work responsibility—my family!

Parallel Search and Adaptation

A third method for tapping your creativity and generating an expansive list of options is parallel search and adaptation. To use this method, actively scan your past and present, your habits at work, your at-home behavior, your friends' lifestyles, the material you read, the television programs you watch—literally anything for ideas you can borrow outright or adapt to suit your needs. The following questions are suggestions for guiding your search. Remember, no matter how simple the solution seems, consider other possibilities.

- What else in my life is like this?
- Is there something I've done or seen before that might be applicable to this situation?
- What can I copy?
- Whom can I emulate?
- What could fit my problem with a few new twists?
- What have I read that is similar to this?
- Of what does my situation remind me?

The use of parallels and adaptation is common in business, writing, music, humor, sports, and television. As Wendell Phillips once noted, "In every matter that relates to invention, to use, or beauty or form, we are borrowers."[20] Every new joke is an old one in disguise; some humorists assert that there are only six basic gags. Goethe maintained that all the stories in the world are constructed from one of 36 basic plots. Willa Cather refuted this, saying, "There are only two or three human stories, and they go on repeating themselves as fiercely as if they had never happened before."[21]

The family portraits included in this book have consistently demonstrated the effectiveness of parallel search and adaptation. Parents have taken bits of one idea and merged them with pieces of another, sometimes simple answers to complex issues in order to design novel solutions. The resources discussed under Roadblock No. 1 in Chapter 4 (time, money, and support) regain their elasticity in the process; the options balloon inflates.

Four commonly used strategies for applying parallel search and adaptation are outlined below, along with examples of how parents have implemented the method.

Applying At-Home Experience to Work

Becky Smythe, a 41-year old R.N. and mother of two, remained at home with her children for three years while her husband Jim, a 42-year old hospice physician, was completing his residency. Becky found that her time at home gave her "a chance to gradually shift my work to reflect current interests and skills." Prior to her stint as a stay-home mother, Becky had worked in an adult clinic and never considered working with a different age population. She told us:

> After the children my first job offer turned out to be in pediatrics, a field for which by then I felt especially suited. My time out of the workforce for full-time child care gave me a chance to get hands-on experience and read a lot about it on my own, all to my ultimate advantage.

Applying Work Experience to Home Life

Becky's husband, Jim, spent three years becoming intimately acquainted with the on-call concept familiar to all residents. He decided subsequently to try the on-call idea at home, and reports it's worked well.

Becky and I set up an on-call schedule on weekends to allow each of us time off as a parent. Our kids had no problem adjusting to the idea and have learned to consult the on-call parent while the other is off duty for a few hours or even an entire day.

The notion of regularly scheduled update appointments is commonplace at work: Half an hour or so every week or two weeks is set aside for colleagues to apprise one another of their activities. One of the fathers we spoke with modified this concept to establish a "telephone time" with his daughter (who, incidentally, had recently discovered the phone and pronounced it her favorite form of communication). Another father designated 7:00 to 7:30 nightly as "just us time" with his son. Sometimes the two ended up lying in bed talking together for half an hour. Other times they played games or read books together.

Remember Diana and Heather Tyler? Heather provided the clue for "just us time" when she told Diana, "Let's pretend you are calling me on the telephone and you will only talk to me."

Most jobs include time for a break in the workday to allow employees to have time away from the job, to do what they prefer. Whether it is a walk, a workout at the gym, lunch, a meeting with a friend or colleague, or shopping, it means time that belongs *exclusively* to you.

The use of "exclusive time" has allowed many working parents we talked with the time they needed to be with other adults, such as spouses, friends, and relatives. One couple arranges to have lunch together in a special restaurant once a week, in order to find time during hectic workdays "to stimulate intimacy." Another couple goes away together, without children, one weekend every three to four months:

Whether it be to the "Big City" for a concert and dinner, or to the seashore for sun and fun, this gives us something to look forward to. It provides for lots of sharing while we plan for our next weekend away. Time together is important. It belongs to just us.

One father plans time to be with his brothers, who live in distant cities, by arranging his business trips to coordinate visits with them at least four times a year.

> Everyone gathers at a central place. We catch up on events, family, and so on. It's all very relaxed and it reminds us of an earlier time. It's a special time because it's exclusive time with people that care very much about each other.

On the same subject, another parent responded with:

> We are so busy taking care of essentials—making money, child rearing, getting ahead—that there is little time to nurture each other and nurture relationships with other adults. People who are always too rushed to have time for each other and friends may expect more from a spouse than is really possible. Maybe it's a reason for the divorce situation. We have time that is just ours—no one can take it away from us.

You're probably saying, "Those are terrific ideas if you have someone to care for your children." The parents we spoke with devised all kinds of cooperative arrangements, especially those who did not have parents or other relatives close by.

The co-ops allowed parents to have "exclusive time" by sharing babysitting, house-sitting, and pet-sitting with other couples. Some parents developed credit and debit systems to ensure that all parents in the co-op would be entitled to "exclusive time" in a way that was satisfying to them.

In response to the concept of co-op arrangements one woman said:

> With the children so young and Keith away all the time, I teamed up with three neighboring families, one in particular with similar-age children and a similar work schedule. We spent many hours at each other's houses while the children played. We talked, shared housework. It was an absolute lifesaver. All advantages and no disadvantages.

Use What You Read or Hear About

> I've always felt strongly that if the shoe doesn't fit, don't
> wear it. Buy a new style, or a different size, or a different
> material—but whatever you do, don't stick to your old shoes
> just because you paid a lot of money for them or want to
> look like everyone else.

Walt Nickerson, a 42-year-old publisher, wasn't giving us his
philosophy on shoe selection; his words were reflections of his
attitude toward life.

> When I was married and my son was 1 or 1½ my wife and
> I decided to hire an in-home babysitter. We advertised, and
> interviewed, and advertised some more and ended up with
> a list of women we labelled acceptable if we were desperate.
> Finally, we sat down and tried to strip away all our precon-
> ceived notions and examine our real alternatives.

One of the ideas that emerged from that session was Walt's shift
away from looking for one full-time caregiver toward seeking two
part-timers.

> I had just read an article about the burnout rate of teachers
> of young children and I thought, ''Maybe we could cut
> down on our caregiver's burnout potential and open up the
> job at the same time to women who weren't looking for full-
> time infant care.

The change in required hours of employment more than doubled
the pool of applicants. Walt and his wife were able to consider
the final result: a 57-year-old mother of three on Mondays
through Thursdays, and a 22-year-old college senior on Fridays
and sometimes during weekends.

> The best part as far as my wife and I were concerned was the
> difference in personality and child-rearing techniques between
> the two. Our son really benefited from the best of each.

David Robertson, the single father you were introduced to in Chapter 2, was keenly aware of the stress placed upon his career and his son Bryan by his attempting to pick Bryan up on time from the child-care center at the end of the day.

> Everything I read told me how important it was to be on time, be consistent. For Bryan it was even more important, for he had already experienced abandonment by one parent. I would be caring for a patient and feeling frustrated when I looked at my watch and it was time to get to the center. The solution came when a friend in another city suggested I ask the child-care center's director if she knew anyone who would be willing to take Bryan home, settle him in, possibly start dinner, and give me the hour leeway I desperately needed. Lucky me, Bryan's teacher was anxious to take on the job to supplement her income. She lived near our home and she really knew Bryan well—what a blessing! I guess, if you never ask, you never know. I'd recommend that other parents with the same dilemma consider the same solution.

Lucy MacFarlane, whom you met in Chapter 4, literally beamed as she related the story of how she found a child-care center in the community she moved to three years ago.

> I started out with the Yellow Pages, asking around, looking on bulletin boards—all the usual things. Then I heard about a child-care fair sponsored by one of the community colleges. It was a take-off on the health fair, job fair, or college day idea, when organizations set up information booths and answer your questions about what they have to offer. All kinds of child-care centers were represented—profit, non-profit, large, small. For me, it was like killing 30 birds with one stone! I was able to talk with so many people that morning and I learned a lot.

Use What's Worked Before; Draw on Your Childhood Experiences
The second youngest in a family of seven, Marlene Scott was accustomed to doing her share around the house. Each child was responsible for his or her room, as well as one other routinely

scheduled task, such as emptying the trash cans, polishing the silver, washing the car, or cleaning the refrigerator. Now, she and her husband and three children engage in a collective activity every Saturday morning for two hours: housecleaning.

> I never felt like it was one person's responsibility to keep the house picked up when I was young; yet when my own children were infants and toddlers, I got into the habit of doing almost everything myself. I was feeling a lot of resentment and that's when Rich and I implemented the family chore-time system *we* grew up with.

Meal preparation is also a shared responsibility. "We started that when the kids reached four years of age," Rich explained. "Each of them planned a menu, prepared as much as possible, and got as much parental help as necessary."

Many people remember the age-old tradition of attending religious services with their families. However, the Martin family has taken that idea and added a new twist:

> Instead of Sunday church, we stay home and have "church." We all help to cook a big brunch together; we sit, eat, and talk. The important part is, everyone shares something special—a poem, a song, or a thought about our family.

Get Involved with Groups

Most Americans have been involved in peer groups at some point in their lives in order to find enjoyment, encouragement, emotional support, advice, and companionship. Some working parents, remembering what worked before, have found a source of strength in forming or being members of groups that allow them to support their work and family life and sometimes provide some form of tangible aid such as help with a new job, transportation, or child care. The groups our parents talked about were different from the anonymous, formal social service organizations that people turn to in times of crisis. Our parents talked of groups with shared interests and common goals.

Joan and Mark Miller, a dual-doctor couple, belong to a national group called Dual-Doctor Families, which provides them with periodic newsletters and updated annotated bibliographies of published material on the subject of dual-doctor families. As a result of their national association, Joan and Mark have formed a small group in their area that meets to discuss the important, unique issues that dual-doctor families face. Mark said:

> We're like all other dual-career families, but we have some special concerns that are part of the medical profession. Meeting with other doctors just getting started in careers and families is great. We want to remain intact while juggling our two lives.

A couple in southern California, Jeff and Julia Sonder, are psychologists sharing a private practice and the care of their children at home. The Sonders started a system of networks at their local church in order "to provide parents with education, support, and encouragement." The Sonders planned, organized, and implemented a program of support services that provides help with child care and transportation, emergency caregivers, home/health visitors,* and a host of other services through a system of lay volunteers who respond to the needs of the parishioners. Because of the positive response to this initial attempt, the Sonders are extending their interest, and are helping other religious organizations start similar networks.

Apply Past Success to New Circumstances

Karen Vandy, the single mother and attorney you met in Chapter 4, described for us her first experience with hiring someone to clean the apartment she lived in before she was married and became a parent:

---

*"Home/health visitors" is a relatively new service, an extension of the visiting nurse service. But home/health visitors are not required to have professional certification.

> I never realized how much it would mean until it was being done for me. Just having the house picked up and the dishes done during the day . . . it meant a lot to be able to come home to a neat house. It was exhilarating to walk in the door at 6:00 P.M. and *not* have to immediately start clearing the dishes from breakfast.

Years later, when Karen was looking for an in-home caregiver for her son, she remembered what a bonus it had been to receive help with the housework.

> I never wanted to give the impression that housework comes before my son, because it didn't and doesn't! But my own sanity was greatly improved if the babysitter would vacuum on Mondays and Fridays, clean the bathroom on Tuesdays, wash the kitchen floor on Thursdays, and throw a load of wash in on Wednesdays. It didn't take that much time. I asked for an hour per day but it was such a help!

Mike Watts, a single parent and an executive in a telecommunications research laboratory, was feeling overwhelmed with a deadline for a major project. Remembering his own college experiences, he was reminded of the time he was taking a statistics course in college and had the opportunity to mesh theory into practice by interning for a local company. Mike contacted several local universities and was able to recruit two students as interns to work on the project. As we talked with Mike it was obvious that he was pleased to be able to apply his own past success to new circumstances.

Where the Creative Flow Can Lead

As you've seen, the creative flow can lead to new options, to old options with a new twist, to whatever combination of original and borrowed ideas suits your needs at work and at home. Creativity gets you around roadblocks so that you can keep moving forward. When you draw on the creative energy that resides in all of us, you can inflate your balloon of options.

6

Supporting Work and the Family: A View from the Workplace

The basic belief found in "excellent" companies is a very real respect for the individual. They don't just say that people are their most important asset—they mean it and show it! The best companies treat people as adults, treat them as partners and treat them with dignity . . . .

—Thomas Peters and Robert Waterman, Jr.
In Search of Excellence

There is an ecological relationship between work and family life, worker and workplace, the health of the corporation and the well-being of the community. For this reason we felt it was necessary to address the balance of work and family not only from the parent-employee perspective, but from the perspective that *many working parents are employers too.* Many of the working parents we interviewed were managers, corporate leaders, entrepreneurs, or other professionals with the capacity to influence the workplace.

122

Employers can make a big difference in helping working parents successfully integrate work and family, thus increasing their productive capacity at work and at home.

If you are an employee, perhaps you can benefit from knowing what some employers in the nation are doing to aid working parents. You may be encouraged to discuss the issues with your co-workers and then form a task force that can present the issues to your employer from a sound and well-informed perspective.

If you are a working parent and also an employer, perhaps this chapter will encourage you to explore the work/family concerns and issues that are unique to your parent-employees, and then be prompted into action!

Coming of Age in Corporate America

While much of corporate America is trying to come of age in the emerging information-processing society, some employers have already come of age in response to the issues that surround the balance of work and family. These are the companies, small and large, that are demonstrating creativity and resourcefulness in order to keep pace with the vast changes in society, in the workplace, and in their employees' own patterns of family life. These are the employers who are keeping step with the Generation with Choices, who recognize that in order to keep up with the present and the future, they need to abandon their patriarchal foothold that is founded on a past that no longer exists in U.S. society.

Trends relating to new work/family patterns have been reported in all the media and are evident throughout the social landscape. Although many people might choose to ignore the trends or pretend that they don't influence their lives, the facts do remain and do have an effect on working parents and their employers.

- Home and family are important parts of the lives of both men and women.

- Women's economic contributions are essential to their families' well-being.
- If husbands and wives have career ambitions, traditional family work patterns must adjust to the new demands.
- Workers in increasing numbers desire major changes in the amount and scheduling of time spent at work.
- Corporations and families compete for working parents' loyalty and devotion. This may stress the family system.
- Employees in increasing numbers expect that companies will do something about their concerns, problems, and complaints.

Some far-sighted employers have a new view of the organization. They recognize the need for the pursuit of excellence at the workplace by demonstrating not only a concern for greater productivity, but also a concern for people. This issue has been considered in major business magazines. Some of America's corporate leaders have said it best:

Organizations cannot separate work and family life, because the success of the system of democratic free enterprise in the United States depends on both.

—Amory Houghton, Jr.
Chairman of the Board
Corning Glass

Employers need to respond to employee needs in order to continually assure that they maintain an available pool of talented workers.

—J. F. McKay
President
Institute for Cancer Research

Happy children plus happy parents equals happy shareholders.

—Leonard Silverman
Vice President for Human Resources
Hoffman LaRoche

Our gain is that hopefully our company will be a place our employees really want to go to—that we can help enrich their lives by the kind of company we run—that they will find a little more happiness on a day-to-day basis because of our work/family policies.

—David Shaw
Operations Manager
Hartstrings, Inc.

When the learning center opened, it changed our way of operating. You bring people to the learning center and their whole attitude towards us becomes, ''If this company is this progressive, then it must be one I want to do business with.''

—Jim Wyllie
President
Nylon Craft Corporation

While there is no Hippocratic oath for businessmen, there is, nevertheless, a compelling responsibility that all of us share, one way or another, in meeting the needs of society. Businesspeople must elevate their vision of the bottom line to embrace social as well as economic goals.

—Arnold Hiatt
President
Stride Rite Corporation

Restructuring the Organization

Run, run, run as fast as you can,
You can't catch me, I'm the Gingerbread Man!

Under the familiar hierarchical corporate system, people raced to the top of the corporate ladder as fast as they could, like the Gingerbread Man in the children's story. But when they got there, too often they forgot that their role was to get things done through people, with people, and for people. This pattern is fast diminishing.

In their best selling book, *Reinventing the Corporation,*[22] John Naisbitt and Patricia Aburdene discuss new ways of defining corporate structures. These redefinitions are decentralized, more human, and more appealing to today's worker than the familiar hierarchical pyramid. According to Naisbitt and Aburdene, "It is as if all the boxes in the organization chart were thrown into the air and programmed to fall into a new set of patterns that best facilitate communication—networks, hubs, lattices, circles and wheels." These creative organization structures provide a new structure that can accommodate working parents—and the organizations that employ them—to help the delicate balance of work and family succeed.

The new kind of organization, as described by Naisbitt and Aburdene, "is based on the mutual interest of the corporation and the people within them. The interconnectedness between the corporation and other aspects of life, education, health, the family and the community means a company can no longer sit back and complain . . ." The new kind of organization they envision will exist as a resource for people. Managers will shift from authoritarian order givers to facilitators, mentors, and developers of human services and human potential. The new values at the workplace will recognize that human beings, not well-oiled machines, can help the organization to flourish or die; that each employee has a personal responsibility for the success of the organization; and that each employer has a responsibility to provide a work environment that is nurturing and satisfying for the employees.

Parents spoke about their desire for a nurturing place to work—one where:

- It's okay to stay home if your child is sick.
- It's okay to work from 7:00 A.M. to 3:00 P.M. for the next one to two years in order to be home with your children.
- You aren't penalized for working at home some days.
- Management doesn't think the employees are trying to get away with as little work as possible.

More Ways to Work: Career Paths That Provide Options

In Chapter 4 we described how corporate America's search for the perfect employee creates roadblocks to the successful integration of work and family. Too many organizations still expect all their employees to adhere to an exploitive career development path, sacrificing all areas of their personal lives in order to be successful in their work lives.

The traditional path to corporate success has always been expected to resemble a rocket taking off, straight up with no detours along the way. This career path may work for some people, but it was not designed to provide options, and it is unrealistic for working parents who have a serious commitment to *both* parenting and working.

The Linear Path

Dr. James Clawson, Professor at the Colgate Darden Graduate School of Business Administration, at the University of Virginia, drew on the findings of Professor Michael Driver of the University of Southern California to depict this traditional approach as the linear path to career success. (See Figure 3.) In this pattern

Figure 3. Linear career path.

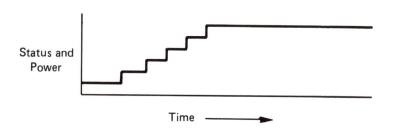

Status and Power

Time ⟶

the individual rises steadily and quickly to power and status in the organization.

Dr. Clawson has noted that not everyone always wants to put professional success first in their lives. Figures 4 and 5 depict several alternate career paths that may encourage the working parent to meet the demands of work and family.

The Spiral Path

Here the individual periodically takes on new challenges but starts over in a relatively elementary status each time, without diminishing the employee's self-worth or value to the company. (See Figure 4.)

The Steady State

This is for the professional who is highly skilled in a field and works in depth without vertical mobility for a sustained period of time—once again, without diminishing the individual's self-worth or value to the organization. (See Figure 5.)

For working parents it may be necessary for the corporation to acknowledge "time out" or "people plateauing" as viable alternatives, without penalty to the employee. Perhaps an individual's success can consist of sometimes following a linear up-

Figure 4. Spiral career path.

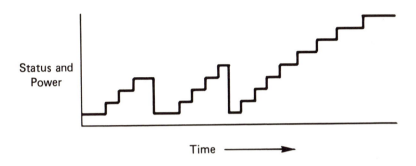

Figure 5. Steady career path.

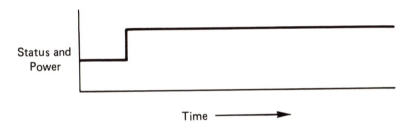

ward path at home and maintaining a steady state at work, and then reversing the two states when appropriate.

The Apprenticeship Scheme

Another alternative approach to employee success, called the apprenticeship scheme, was suggested by Lotte Bailyn in *Accommodation of Work to Family: Analysis of Couples with Two Careers.*[25] Here employers would by word and deed provide a longer time period for career people to make it in the corporate hierarchy, giving them an ''apprenticeship'' before measuring their level of productivity. This would certainly allow working parents the opportunity to compete more equally with individuals who are not parents. This model has the potential to prevent burnout among working parents who are trying to do it all at once.

If workers are not taught that more than one model for success at work can exist, many can never feel really comfortable about the job they are doing at home or at work. Many companies are proposing developmental models for career success that aim at protecting their employees' work lives and personal lives. They are doing this by acknowledging a couple of significant facts. It is okay to sustain more than one kind of career path and success can be measured in more than one way.

IBM holds seminars for people who are vital to the organization but may not be on the fast track. The seminars aim to assure the self-esteem of the individual. The organization tries to make clear that it defines success in terms of satisfaction: doing the present job well and the understanding that moving up the career ladder is not the only way to feel successful.

Companies such as Kodak, Xerox, and Hewlett Packard also understand the need to manage personnel in a way that protects their personal lives as well as work lives. They renegotiate personnel contracts when necessary, disclaim the work ethic that urges people to work until they drop, and treat people as a resource by appreciating creativity and providing an environment that stimulates personal growth.

Five Ways Employers Can Help Parent-Employees

Restructuring the organization and providing more options for career paths will benefit the entire workforce, including parent-employees. There are many additional ways for employers to get involved in helping the working parents in their organizations to merge work life and family life. Employers who have a growing awareness of social responsibility—and who recognize that to survive in a global economy, they have to be on the top of social as well as economic trends—are implementing family-supportive policies in a number of ways that may be helpful for you to know.

As we mentioned in Chapter 1, we are not going to include vast detail about employer initiatives for child care in this book. Instead, we will briefly outline some of the ways you—the employer and parent-employee—can become involved, give a few examples of success stories from the working parents we interviewed, and then direct you to the Annotated Bibliography and Resource Organizations for additional sources of information. (See Appendixes B and C.)

Employers can assist working parents in five major ways: education and support programs; flexible personnel policies; financial assistance programs; direct child-care services; and advocacy of public policies supporting children, working parents, and families.

Education and Support Programs

Because the merger of work and family is a complex issue, working parents need as much information and education as possible. Employers can sponsor such programs as:

- Working parent seminars
- Information and referral programs
- Working parent task forces
- Working parent counseling services

All are ways to help parent-employees alleviate stress, anxiety, and frustration by increasing their understanding of their dual roles and their ability to control their lives. Such programs also help establish networks of people who have similar interests and concerns.

Flexible Personnel Policies

Most organizations provide standard benefits to employees such as vacation time, sick leave, and health and life insurance plans. Few benefit plans include considerations for child care. Flexible personnel policies would include such items as:

- Flexible work times for full-time employees
- Permanent part-time employment *with* benefits
- Job sharing
- Work-at-home options
- Cafeteria benefit plans that would allow employees to se-lect benefits most helpful to their families at the time.
- Family-oriented sick leave policies
- Adequate maternity and paternity leaves

Such personnel policies give working parents far more flexibility to arrange their complicated and varying lifestyles, and are especially helpful with events such as the birth of a baby or the illness of a child.

Financial Assistance Programs

One of the overwhelming problems that working parents face is the cost or lack of quality care for their children. To help ease the burden employers could consider:

- Vendor programs that involve the purchase of child-care slots in existing community child-care programs. The organization can usually purchase the slots at reduced cost and then offer them to their parent-employees.
- Vouchers to help defray the cost of child-care centers.
- Flexible spending accounts allowing working parents to request that money be withheld from their income to establish a child-care account. Parent-employees then set up their own child-care reimbursement plan. This arrangement helps working parents because income withheld in this manner is *not* taxed, so employees receive higher net pay after taxes. This benefit is often part of a flexible personnel plan.
- Corporate contributions to nonprofit child-care programs, which help increase the quality and quantity of child-care programs.

Employers who provide financial assistance are helping working parents without getting directly involved with child care. Financial assistance programs may be attractive to an employee workforce that is very diverse and perhaps interested in a variety of child-care arrangements.

Direct Child-Care Services

Organizations can directly establish and support several types of child-care programs, including:

- Worksite child-care centers, where one employer establishes a child-care center near or at the workplace.
- Child-care consortiums, where several employers join to establish a child-care program for the parent-employees of all consortium members.
- Before- and after-school programs, where an employer supports a local child-care program, school district, or summer camp to accommodate the needs of working parents with school-age children.
- Sick-child-care programs, where an employer contributes to or establishes a program to accommodate the needs of working parents when their children are ill.
- Family day-care networks, where the employer trains and monitors people who run family day-care homes for small groups of children.

An employer's direct involvement in child-care services is very helpful to parent-employees, but it involves much commitment and more time and money than some organizations may be willing to incur. What is important is that employers become involved in some way to help working parents balance work and family so that they need not walk a tightrope each day.

Advocacy of Public Policies Supporting Children, Working Parents, and Families

The United States is the only advanced industrialized nation without public policies that support families, working parents, and children as part of its national agenda. Employers could make a difference by:

- Encouraging elected officials to take political action that supports families.
- Encouraging local school districts to implement after-school programs for school-age children.
- Lobbying through business and professional groups for a public policy on paid maternity and paternity leaves, and for work scheduling that synchronizes better with family lives.

Success Stories: Employers Who Are Leading the Parade

There is the story of an old Chinese philosopher who imparted his wisdom to his young students, "When you see a parade, you have three choices: You can join it, get out of the way, or get out in front and lead it." Some organizations are getting out in front and leading the parade by allowing work and family to be viewed as a shared experience, not as confrontational forces. These organizations are examining their options and creating solutions that may make a difference to the life of the company and to the lives of their employees. It is this desire to lead the parade that can make the work/family connection possible.

"Part of Our Employees' Extended Family"

The operations manager at Hartstrings (first introduced in Chapter 2) was eager to talk about the responsibility of the organization to its employees. He recognized that:

While the term 'entrepreneurial' is now in vogue, small companies—Mom and Pop companies—have always existed in the United States, and it is just these kinds of companies that have contributed to much of the economic and human growth in the United States.

When Peggy and Bruce Earle opened their first Hartstrings facility outside of the Earle home, a major consideration was child care for Andy (then 1½). A workable solution was to bring a babysitter to Hartstrings to care for Andy and a six-month-old child of another Hartstrings employee. Peggy and Bruce felt that "a babysitter at the worksite was the best of all worlds"—someone to care for their child so that they could conduct their business and monitor Andy's daily activities at the same time.

Peggy soon gave birth to Timmy. Timmy spent most of his first months in a cradle next to Mom's and Dad's adjoining desks. Peggy could nurse Timmy, Peggy and Bruce could attend to their other needs, and if a really important meeting was coming up, they could turn Timmy over to the babysitter.

As Hartstrings grew, so did the child-care concerns and arrangements of Hartstrings' employees. The babysitting service grew into a child-care center at Hartstrings, and most Hartstrings parent-employees had their children enrolled in the center "because of convenience, low cost, and the family atmosphere that prevailed."

In 1986, when Hartstrings once again moved to a newer, larger, and more modern facility, the child-care center moved too. The new Hartstrings Child Development Center includes space for sick-child care, infant care, toddler care, and after-school care. Its philosophy recognizes the importance of a stable, secure, nurturing environment for children, and its most important goal is the successful merger of work and family life that will complement the family, not to be a substitute for the family.

The Hartstrings Child Development Center is an ambitious project prompted by a youthful, entrepreneurial zeal. The Earles can identify with their employees and have the luxury of establishing the traditions at Hartstrings.

Peggy and Bruce's son Andy is now ready for first grade, so he will not be spending much time in the Child Development Center, except for after-school care. Timmy, the Earles' youngest child, is ready for a preschool program elsewhere; nevertheless, the Earles are forging ahead with plans for the new Child Development Center "because we are committed to the idea that our company is one part of our employees' extended family, and the care of employees' children is a natural outgrowth of that philosophy."

Helping Parents Help Themselves

Some of the working parents we interviewed, employers and employees alike, found that strengthening a family's ability to help themselves through family-responsive work policies and practices was the best kind of support employers could provide for their parent-employees.

"I feel better already," echoed one parent at the conclusion of the second of a six-part series of working parent seminars held at her place of employment, a county government agency.

The working parent seminars were sponsored by the employer for small groups of working parents, with 12 to 15 employees meeting for a period of 1½ hours during lunch hour. They were the employer's first attempt at "helping working parents to help themselves" through information gathering, networking, support building, and constructive problem solving. "The focus of the seminars is education, not therapy," said the seminar leaders.

The responses from the parents in attendance were very positive:

- Just two meetings helped me realize that I was spending a lot of valuable time placing blame for feeling badly on people at work and on my own family. I felt boxed in. I couldn't even think of ways to be more efficient, more relaxed, and happier. Through education at the seminars, I learned about eliminating the time spent on blaming others for my life's stresses and everyday problems. It made a difference in my life. I think I now have some insight and I can be more constructive.

- It sure is encouraging to know I could actually learn to manage my time, that it was actually possible to make time for me too.

By enhancing working parents' ability to feel in control of their lives and by acknowledging their parental concerns and the isolation often felt by families, family-responsive policies and practices can make a powerful contribution toward helping employees balance work and family life. This benefits the employer as well.

The message given to the employees at the working parent seminars we attended was made clear to us by the seminar participants:

- At least we know this organization has some idea of what we [working parents] are going through trying to juggle two lives. At least we feel that people here care.
- We all had the same problems—managers, secretaries. Somehow it made all of us seem more human. Next time my superior is nasty, I'll remember that he probably had a rough day at home or at work.

A young, newly divorced mother in Florida told us that the employer-initiated work/family policy at her organization "saved my life."

It took most of my married life to conceive my child, and three weeks following the birth of my daughter, my husband left, just walked out and wasn't heard from for a year. I was devastated. I had to get back to work and I desperately needed child care. I was confused and frightened.

I was able to get a job at a nearby hospital and was so grateful when I discovered that right in the hospital was a woman who helped parents to find child care. I visited with her. I told her what my predicament was and she assured me she could help. She referred me to a few child-care cen-

ters—some close to my home, some that were near to
work—told me how much they cost, checked to see which
child-care centers had openings for an infant, and then ad-
vised me to visit *all* the centers.

In three days I made my decision, and I was ready to go to
work. I felt in control of my life. I wasn't helpless any more.
It was difficult for a long time, but never impossible. I don't
know what I would have done without the hospital's help
with my child-care problem. And I didn't have to pay a fee
for the service.

The same attitude, that of support for working parents, has
been shown to me by my boss. He understands that if my
daughter is sick, I may need to stay home; he understands
if occasionally I have to leave work a few minutes early. I
guess it is because he too is divorced. He is young and
realizes how tough life can get some days for a working
parent.

The hospital referred to in this story is the Morton Plant Hospital
in Panellas County, Florida. We spoke with the director of the
Child Care Connection, an information and referral service set
up by the hospital in 1983 to help its parent-employees with
child-care concerns and issues. It is a benefit offered to all employees and currently serves an estimated 100 parents a year.

We asked the assistant director of the program, why the
program was implemented. She told us:

It was a response to employee needs. Some of the hospital's
first thoughts were to open a worksite child-care center, but
the cost of starting up a center, plus the belief that an information and referral service could serve a greater number
of employees, prompted the start-up of the Child Care Connection.

The information and referral service includes help to parents in locating quality child care, either in a family day-care
home or in a center. It also includes ongoing screening, monitoring, supervision, and evaluation of all child-care providers that
are registered with Child Care Connection. (The fee for child-

care providers is $25.00 per year.) The director and her assistant visit each child-care setting once or twice a month to continually assess the quality of the participating child-care programs and each child's progress. The director then provides each parent-employee with a written report about his or her child. In addition, Child Care Connection sponsors a toy- and book-lending library available to all child-care providers participating in the program, which enhances the curriculum.

Another component of the information and referral service at Morton Plant Hospital is the Saturday morning coffee hour, designed to bring working parents together to share ideas, concerns, and information about child development and parenting.

A Joint Venture

Kathy Gillis is a working mother. She is married and has two children, Danny (1½) and Beth (2½). The Gillis family lives in a single-family home in a suburban Northeastern community, close to where Kathy grew up. She told us:

> I need to work. I can't always count on my husband's seasonal employment to provide the security we need for our family. I also need independence—the feeling that I can accomplish something.

Armed with determination, tenacity, a winning personality, and little training, Kathy applied for a position in the research and development division of a midsize corporate conglomerate. She was hired as a line worker in a pilot program. While working on the line, Kathy was identified by the technical director as a "hard-working, capable employee" with skill and tenacity. As a result she was promoted to a position in the quality control division, with the technical director assuming the role of training Kathy in her new position. Kathy continued to be a valuable and talented employee.

My new job provided me with a sense of accomplishment
and the training I never had earlier. It gave me a new
perspective—I knew I wanted something more for my
children than my husband and I had. The future seemed
brighter.

All was going well for Kathy and her family until her child-
care arrangements became a problem. Kathy's sister, who had
been caring for Danny and Beth along with her own child, had
to seek outside employment because of financial problems. At
the same time, Kathy's mother got sick and couldn't take over
the child-care arrangements, as she had in the past. Kathy's husband was in the peak period at his job as a construction worker,
so he couldn't fill in as the primary caregiver. Kathy became
concerned and depressed over the possibility of having to leave
her job. She thought about working part time, taking a temporary leave, or putting her children in a child-care center.
However, the options all seemed to present other important
problems—loss of income or an increase in cost to the family.

Kathy went to talk with the technical director, hoping for
some suggestions for a solution to her child-care problem. After
much discussion, the technical director referred the problem to
the president of the company. Though many readers will not
believe it, the president called Kathy to his office, discussed her
family concerns with her, and then to Kathy's surprise negotiated a "joint venture." The president suggested that because
Kathy was a valuable employee who had recently been trained
to perform a job that was important to the company, and because
there were no established family-responsive personnel policies
that covered Kathy's situation, he would provide her with a
voucher that would guarantee her $50.00 per week, to be paid
directly to a licensed child-care center to help cover the cost of
child care for her two children, providing Kathy would stay on
at the company.

A problem Kathy then encountered was finding immediate
openings for two children at a quality child-care center. The
president of the organization, sincere about the joint agreement,

took another step. He contacted the early childhood division of a local college, and with its help was able to locate a child-care center that would establish a working relationship with the company. The center agreed to enroll Kathy's two children, in exchange for a "donation of needed materials and supplies from the corporation and the promise of additional enrollments if all went well."

This arrangement meant that Kathy could stay on at her job and her children would be well taken care of at the child-care center. Kathy not only was grateful for the child-care arrangements the company had helped her work out, but told us,

> My children are benefiting from child care in special ways. They are with wonderful people, learning many things from other people that I couldn't or wouldn't be able to expose them to. I think they are getting more training and education at the child-care center that can help them in the future.

A Growing Child-Care Consortium

"It's the only humane thing to do," said David Robertson in response to our question about the employer-supported child-care center his son Bryan attends. "If employers expect to have workers that are dedicated and productive, they need to address the family needs of employees." David feels that he and Bryan are both benefiting from the child-care center.

> Bryan is being well taken care of in a safe, clean, and secure environment, where people are loving and allow him to be a little boy. For me the child-care center is a source of support, too. It is a place where I know my child is okay, where there are the structure and patterns of daily activities that every child needs, and it provides me with feedback about how my child is doing. Also it's a place where people understand *you* and *your* child.

The employer-supported child-care center Bryan attends was the brainchild of the executive vice president at one of the health-care institutions involved in the child-care consortium. The executive vice president recognized the need to attract and maintain talented workers, and a child-care center was one way of accomplishing this. This executive convinced three other health-care institutions, in close proximity to his institution, to join him in sharing equally the start-up costs for the center, and any yearly operating costs that were over and above the annual budget. The center has been in operation for five years, has been very successful, and has grown enough to warrant moving from its original location to a larger facility.

Parent-employees pay monthly tuition based on a sliding fee scale that is determined by their yearly income and other family variables. The total tuition collected is subsidized by the contributing health-care institutions, in order to keep tuitions at an affordable rate.

The most significant problem at the center is the long waiting list. Even with expansion there is not enough space to accommodate all the children of all parent-employees. Children are accepted at the center on a first-come, first-served basis, except perhaps in crisis situations such as the one David was in when he started working for the organization.

Several other issues confront the center. There is a need for 24-hour child care to accommodate all work shifts at the hospital, and for sick-child care to accommodate the parents who must be at work while a child is recuperating from an illness and is not well enough to be part of normal center activities. Also, some parents feel they are subsidizing the center to a greater degree than others by paying a higher tuition rate. Still, the parents are grateful that the center is available to them and told us, ''The employer-supported child-care center makes working and parenting a lot simpler.''

These stories from the workplace have provided a mere glimpse at what is taking place with organizations around the nation in response to the changing needs of parent-employees. The working parents we interviewed were obviously a small sample of the total number of working parents in the nation. However, if they were a representative sample, as we believe they were, their stories provide considerable evidence that organizations are becoming more sensitive to the work/family concerns of their employees, and that a greater percentage of employers are leading the work/family parade than we had thought.

What's in It for the Employer?

A good deal has been written recently that attempts to quantify the financial cost-benefit issues of employer involvement in the concerns of working parents. Attempts have been made to justify financial expenditures for working-parent programs by analyzing the bottom line of an organization's annual report. It has been difficult for many organizations to justify financial expenditures for working-parent initiatives solely on the basis of financial gain—something most employers are accustomed to as part of normal business practices.

According to a 1983 American Management Association report, employers have said that the benefits of programs for working parents far outweigh the costs. In 1982, companies such as PCA in North Carolina, Intermedics in Texas, Sioux Valley Hospital in South Dakota, and Neuville-Mobil Sox in North Carolina were reported by the National Employer-Supported Child Care study to estimate considerable declines in absenteeism, turnover, and tardiness as a result of family-responsive practices. Still, to date there have not been sufficient cost-benefit data to prompt most employers to action.

In our effort to help employers find answers, we are looking in the wrong place if we focus *only* on financial auditing systems. Standard accounting methods cannot measure some kinds of success. Measuring the gain achieved by a new piece of equipment is far easier than measuring the gain from establishing personnel policies that allow parents—men and women—to stay home with sick children when necessary, to take a maternity or paternity leave, or to work at home when possible. Accomplishments dealing with major social issues may have to be measured in non-quantitative terms and over a long period of time.

Organizations need to implement multidimensional social auditing systems that emphasize not only increased profit for stockholders, but also quality of life, the interdependence of people working in a system that requires cooperation, and a balance of social and economic returns.

As the Dow Jones average soared above the 1900 mark, economic analysts told the public that we could no longer use the same tried and true methods for determining the what and why of the economic future of organizations, because society and the organization within society no longer exist the way people remember them, and they do not necessarily abide by the old rules. As one financial analyst indicated, ''We've had too much orthodoxy among the financial intelligentsia—they've been thinking entirely in terms of the usual.''

The American family and the American workforce are also no longer the way employers remember them, and therefore the old, tried and true employee benefit programs no longer meet the needs of today's employees. Employers have much to gain from implementing family-responsive policies and programs, even if, at first glance, some of the gains are intangible. Improved morale and public image are important and do indirectly affect the bottom line.

Family-responsive employers also gain the knowledge that they are helping to shape not only a secure economic society, but also a society whose foundations are valued: secure, safe children, and parents who need and want to work. This is the kind of society that all of us want to be part of, the kind of society where business *and* families can thrive. Ultimately what strengthens the underlying fabric of American society will strengthen the American business community as well.

7

To the Future of Working Families

The life course is not fixed; but widely flexible. It varies with social change—not only the changing nature of the family, the school, the workplace, the community, but also with changing ideas, values, and beliefs. As each new generation . . . enters the stream of history, the lives of its members are marked by the imprint of social change and in time leave their own imprint.

—Jesse Bernard
The Future of Motherhood

In our quest to pronounce judgment on the future, specifically the future of American families who are integrating work and family in their lives, we have been told of the imminent death of the family and of the perils that have befallen the family. We, however, remain optimistic. After interviewing families and employers around the nation, we conclude that *American families are alive and well!*

A Sense of Commitment

We agree that the working families who shared the intimate details of their lives with us are different from those we remember from our own childhoods and those of centuries past; but in no way are the fundamental commitment, concern, and caring of modern families different from those felt by our ancestors. The people we talked with care a good deal about their families. They feel a strong need for a satisfying family life and are committed to being good parents.

We heard many comments from families expressing their commitment and caring:

- I'd rather be a single parent than a nonparent.
- We were pregnant together, not just me, and together we will share in the joys of bringing up Ben.
- The time we spend with Alex is quality. At the end of the day, when there are no more calls to be made, we focus 100 percent on Alex—it's wonderful. I think we get a lot of quality time. I know when my Dad came home from work, he would just read the paper and fall asleep. That was not quality at any time.
- As long as there is love, so that our children know we love them and we know we love each other, that is what is important.
- We hope our children will know that they were loved, respected, and encouraged; that we know the meaning of love and discipline in their lives, and as parents we could admit our own weaknesses; that we worked, played, and grew together.
- It's the most important thing to me that my child grow up happy, secure, and with a good sense of self-worth. I want a happy family, even when he is grown—a circle of love, support, and caring.

The families we met represent a patchwork of complex family patterns. These families are devising new, creative ways to meet their individual family needs in a changing society. Working parents are creating new brands of loyalties, traditions, values, and beliefs that attempt to integrate the old traditions with the new in order to achieve a harmony between their work and family lives.

The working parents and employers we have come to know are helping play vital roles in shaping the future of work life and family life. A *Working Mother* article about changes in real-life couples commented, "Change is usually painful for the individual. But God, does it improve the species."[23] Improving the species may not be the immediate goal of the working parents and employers we met, but many of them are certainly contributing to the improvement of the species in ways we cannot yet evaluate. They are accomplishing this by taking risks, defrosting their creativity, overcoming roadblocks, and devising solutions for linking work and family.

Spreading Ripples of Change

The working families of today are performing in ways that gradually change society, similar to the game of tossing a pebble into a pond and watching the ripples move away from the place where the pebble first fell. This act, however, is translated into a courageous one when traditional cultural and societal messages remind working parents: "Do Not Throw Pebbles into the Pond."

And yet society simultaneously provides the pebbles by encouraging women to be learners and earners, as well as homemakers. Economic trends encourage the creation of dual-earner families. Our culture encourages the concept of freedom, which implies that one has choices. As more people have thrown more pebbles into the pond despite society's mixed messages, we wanted to know how they felt about it. We asked the people we interviewed about the advantages and disadvantages of the family arrangements they have worked out. From single parents we heard:

- I work for less pay, but in return I have time with my children. We have so many wonderful experiences we share.

- I left the field, from social service to corporate America. I was mostly influenced by the idea of earning an income beyond living day to day, and having flexible time to spend with my children.

- I now work smarter, not harder. I proved to my boss I could do it [manage both work and family]. As a result I have less time for me, but more for my children. We are a team.

From dual-earner families we heard:

- I work because we want a particular lifestyle. I would never sacrifice our son for personal goals. He is first.

- By working prior to pursuing my Ph.D. and having a child, I was able to save money, so now I have the economic freedom to work or not to work. Also I feel I'm pulling my weight financially when I am working. This is extremely important to me.

- In deciding to work part time, I feel okay. I'll be working at my career for about 30 to 40 years, so hopefully a slower pace now shouldn't be a problem in the long run.

- The disadvantages [in dual-earner families] are our high expectations. The advantages are the opportunities for us to change jobs, take time off from work, and have more financial independence.

- The big advantage in both nursing and writing is that they lend themselves to part-time or full-time hours, which allows me to work in accordance with the changes in my family.

- Initially I was hindered because of the great demands on time during my training. Recently I have been able to work flexible time. This facilitates planning and family time.

- When I have worked less than full time I used it to enhance my career, to develop skills and gain experience.

The need to continue finding new ways to integrate work and family extends beyond a mere desire to move with the tide, to be a pioneer, or to help write a new definition of family and work. It is based on the knowledge that we can't go home again, at least not to the same place we once knew, where Moms stayed home cooking chicken soup, Dads were gone most of the day at a mystical place called "work," and employers demanded all of their employees' loyalty to the job.

New Choices and Opportunities

The journey toward the integration of work and family is not always a smooth one; sometimes it traverses rocky roads and detours. But working families will succeed. The opportunities for men and women to explore all aspects of their lives, to broaden their repertoire of experiences and behaviors, to share in loving and nurturing, and to perform meaningful work for which they receive psychic as well as economic rewards—all these will help them to survive the journey. Also, the opportunities for working men and women to develop new attitudes about themselves and each other, new commitments, and a new way of finding personal fulfillment so that they don't look back after a lifetime of parenting and working to roads not taken will enable them to succeed. There is no one perfect path or perfect solution for today's men and women. The road is strewn with choices—and opportunities for innovation and creativity.

The ability to make choices affects not only our personal lives but organization lives as well. The organization now has the capacity to benefit from the creative employees who are integrating work and family. These men and women will bring new meaning to their work and will demonstrate not only a desire for economic rewards but a way of finding satisfaction and fulfillment on the job that will enhance the American workplace.

The workplace has the capacity to not be a "thing apart," but a meaningful part of an individual's life, as employers make choices about changes in work patterns, in family-responsive work policies and practices, and in attitudes that enhance the integration of work life and personal life.

It's good business sense for employers to get involved in issues relating to work and family. Not getting involved in clearing roadblocks for working parents can only decrease employee job satisfaction and productivity at the workplace. This would reduce our position not only as a dominant world power in an emerging world economy, but—more important—as a nation truly committed to the family.

The parents we interviewed were not extraordinary, but they were very special. They didn't have it all, nor did most of them expect to. They were like families at any time in American history—sometimes sad, sometimes stressed, sometimes overworked, sometimes angry, sometimes tired, sometimes confused, and many times optimistic and happy. The working parents we met with want the same thing for the future of their children that parents throughout the ages have always wanted.

- I try to teach my children that they can be anything they want to be. There are no limitations except hard work.
- The thing is—you know what's really important is what Billy will say when he's interviewed 30 years from now about his family. "You know, we might not have had everything, but my Mom and Dad were great and they were there when I needed them." That's more important to me than anything else.
- I want my children to be happy (whatever that is), to have successful relationships, to be creative and productive adults. I also hope they will be responsible parents and do the best they can.
- I hope my child will have a fulfilling adulthood with a stable relationship and children. I hope my child will say we helped her to be an independent loving person and that she enjoyed growing up.

- We would like our children to know they are the most important people in our lives and always will be.
- I hope my girls both feel that they have choices in their lives and that they know how to choose the best for themselves and their families.
- I hope my child will work, be a parent, and be anything else he truly wants.

So we come to the end of our journey together. We have witnessed where the American family has been and have caught a glimpse of the Generation with Choices. We have witnessed working parents who truly want to overcome their societal, cultural, and personal roadblocks. They are attempting to balance their work and family lives by devising creative solutions to provide a satisfying life for their children and themselves. They need to work for the fulfillment of a life's dream: providing security for their families and making the balance of work and family succeed. They have a commitment to being alive and well in contemporary America.

We have learned a good deal from the working parents we talked with. We want to offer a toast to them:

> To the future of working families:
> You have taken the road "less traveled by."
> We wish you well, and
> We know you will make the difference.

Appendix A

How Well Is my Child-Care Arrangement Working?

Quality child care is one of the most significant issues working parents must deal with each day, the one most often cited by working parents as causing them the most concern.

Many excellent checklists for selecting a child-care center, child-care provider, or group home can be found in some of the books listed in the Annotated Bibliography. (See Appendix B.) We have elected to include another kind of checklist for working parents here, one that looks at child care from the perspective of the parent, the child, and the caregiver. We believe that in order for child-care arrangements to work, the working parent needs to take all three perspectives into account: How do *I* feel about my child-care arrangements? What is my caregiver's perspective? How is my child responding?

This checklist includes three separate sections to help you answer these questions. The checklist is intended not only to help you determine *your* satisfaction with your child-care arrangements, but also to help increase your awareness of and sensitivity to the *total* child-care picture. It may be helpful to jot down reasons for some of your answers, and to note areas that need further investigation or improvement.

From the Parent's Perspective

These questions will help you choose a caregiver and also monitor and evaluate your current caregiver arrangements. The questions are equally appropriate whether you have an in-home caregiver or are involved with a center-based caregiver. (For grammatical simplicity, we're assuming that the caregiver is a woman, though that certainly isn't always the case.)

1. Do I feel comfortable with my child's caregiver?
   - Can I talk openly about my child?
   - Is she aware of *my* needs as well as my child's?
   - Is she communicating with me and my child about interests, choices, and concerns?
2. Do I know what's going on while my child is outside my care?
   - Do the caregiver and I talk regularly about my child's progress?
   - Do I trust my caregiver's judgment? Do I think she's competent, not just from a custodial viewpoint, but from a developmental one?
3. Does the caregiver carry out her job in accordance with my philosophy of:
   - Child development?
   - Discipline?
   - Nutrition?
   - Time structure?
   - Reinforcement versus punishment?

4. Does the caregiver demonstrate that she really *cares* for my child? Or is this "just a job"?

5. Is my caregiver in excellent physical and mental health?

6. Is my caregiver engaged in any other occupation in addition to the care of my child? If so, how does this affect the quality care of my child?

7. Is this arrangement a hassle—too much commuting, inflexible hours, too costly?

8. Does my caregiver demonstrate a positive attitude toward my child and me? Does my caregiver appear to be relaxed and free of anxiety?

9. Does my caregiver appear to show empathy, and does she act purposefully in interactions with my child?

10. Does my caregiver engage my child in a variety of activities? Are the activities free of bias—that is, are boys involved in domestic activities and girls involved in active, assertive activities?

11. Does my caregiver know what to expect from children at different ages?

12. When all is said and done, do I have a warm, good feeling about my child-care arrangements?

13. After reviewing the next two sections of the questionnaire, am I satisfied that this arrangement is working well for all three parties involved?

From the Child's Perspective

We do not expect that you will ask your child to answer all the following questions; in some instances you can more effectively observe the answers yourself. Either way, these questions are meant to help you focus on your child's perspective, particularly his or her social, emotional, and cognitive development.

1. Am I usually happy and eager to be with the caregiver? Am I comfortable with my caregiver?

2. Am I demonstrating behaviors and competencies that help my parents to feel confident that I am growing and developing according to the best of my ability? (The items listed in this category will vary with the age of your child.)

   - Am I developing self-care skills (toilet training, dressing, undressing)?
   - Am I learning to cope with the world around me?
   - Am I happy and satisfied *most* of the time?
   - Am I developing my own personality?
   - Am I acquiring information about myself, other people, things, and occurrences?
   - Am I communicating with others?
   - Am I developing positive attitudes and problem-solving abilities?
   - Am I demonstrating good play habits? Can I play alone and with others too?
   - Can I work independently for a reasonable amount of time?
   - Can I stay with the task at hand?
   - Am I discovering many new things each day because my caregiver encourages me to do this?

3. Does my caregiver help set limits for my behavior?
4. Is my caregiver sensitive to my feelings and needs:
   - When I cry?
   - When I am angry, upset, or frustrated?
   - When I'm bored?
   - When I'm hungry?
   - When I'm lonely?
   - When I go from one activity to the next?
   - When I need to have my diaper changed or use the toilet?
5. Does my caregiver think I'm a special person? (I know from how she acts.)

6. Do I have many things to keep me busy each day:
   - Walks?
   - Visits to interesting places?
   - Books, blocks, crafts, toys, puzzles?
   - Art, music?
   - Quiet time?
   - Cooking?
   - Friends?
   - Playground?

From the Caregiver's Perspective

Many parents bemoan the fact that caregivers come and go, but perhaps part of the problem is that no one ever asks the caregiver, ''What do *you* think?'' These questions can help you put yourself in the caregiver's shoes, or they can be used as a format for self-evaluation by your caregiver. Once again, the checklist can be used for an in-home caregiver as well as a center-based caregiver.

1. Am I treated with respect by my employer?
2. Am I paid enough for this work?
3. Can I grow in this job? (Are there any opportunities for new learning, competency training, and so on?)
4. Do the parents or my employer (center) give me flexibility in how I carry out my job?
5. Does my employer provide (or do I have) the necessary facilities and equipment to do my job well?
6. Do my daily activities match my job description? (Am I doing what I was hired to do?)
7. Can I communicate openly with parents about concerns and issues as they relate to the child?
8. Are my suggestions valued by the parents?
9. Do I strive for excellence in my job?

10. Does my employer provide rewards for a job well done?
11. Does my employer provide a reasonable system of support?
12. Do the parents plan with me for the optimum growth and development of the child?
13. Does my employer expect that I will succeed?

Appendix B

An Annotated Bibliography of Relevant Readings for Working Parents

In the past ten years there has been a proliferation of publications dealing with topics of interest to working parents: child-care options and selection; child care and family policy; parenting and child-rearing theories; changing roles and responsibilities of mother and father, husband and wife, parent and child; and the impact of employer practices and attitudes on working parents. The selections listed here were chosen in an effort to provide you with additional exposure to published materials relevant to the merger of work and family lives. The exclusion of a publication from the list does *not* imply a negative judgment of its merit or utility.

The selected readings have been organized into six general topics of interest to ensure greater ease in locating necessary information. Many of the published materials fit into more than one category, so we placed publications in the category we believe will be most beneficial as a reference.

Section 1, "Child-Care and Family Policy," contains books and articles on the position of child care and family in U.S. public policy. The history of child care in the United States is outlined, and U.S. child-care and family policy is contrasted with policies adopted by other industrialized nations.

Section 2, "Two-Career Families," addresses the division of child care and domestic responsibilities between dual-career couples. It emphasizes the importance of planning and strong organizational skills to reduce stress and increase household management efficiency, and suggests methods to bring about a more egalitarian division of parental and household responsibilities.

Section 3, "Changing Roles of Mothers and Fathers," focuses on the changing roles of men and women in society, the importance of the participation of both mothers and fathers in the lives of their children, and the effects of paternal employment on children.

Section 4, "Child-Care Selection Guidelines," explains child-care options, identifies the pros and cons of each, and gives advice on how to select the appropriate child-care arrangement and how to find it in your community.

Section 5, "Working Parents," includes comprehensive how-to reference sources targeted for working parents. Contains information on child care and household and time management, and emphasizes the necessity of role clarification within marriage and parent-child relationships.

Section 6, "Changing Work Environments," reviews the role of the employer in facilitating (or hindering) the merger of work and family lives. Several of the references examine the feasibility and existence of alternative work patterns and benefit plans that acknowledge new family structures and working parents' needs.

Section 1: Child-Care and Family Policy

Hardyment, C. *Dream Babies: Three Centuries of Good Advice on Child Care.* New York: Harper & Row, 1983.
An entertaining and informative history chronicling the rise and fall of theories concerning child rearing, from the eighteenth century to today. Helpful in restoring perspective on the often overwhelming and conflicting range of child-care advice.

Kamerman, S.B. "Child Care and Family Benefits: Policies of Six Industrialized Countries." *Monthly Labor Review,* Vol. 103, (November 1980), pp. 23–28.
Reviews the different types of benefits available to help working parents cope with their dual roles in France, Sweden, Hungary, East and West Germany, and the United States. Considers the implications of income transfers, child-care services, and different employment policies, and concludes that adaptations in these areas should be the focus of more attention in the United States.

_____ . *Parenting in an Unresponsive Society.* Riverside, N.J.: The Free Press, 1980.
An in-depth study of the day-to-day coping mechanisms displayed by employed women, including child-care management, household and family management, and dealing with work-related problems. Concludes with policy recommendations for child-care alternatives and working-parents benefits, as well as a report on child-care facilities in France and Sweden.

Keniston, K., and The Carnegie Council on Children. *All Our Children: The American Family Under Pressure.* San Diego: Harcourt Brace Jovanovich, 1977.
Report on the social and economic crises faced by American families and recommends issues for a national family policy.

Roby, P., ed. *Child-Care—Who Cares?* New York: Basic Books, 1975.
A collection of articles on child-care programs and child-care policy.

Select Committee on Children, Youth, and Families. *Families and Child Care: Improving the Options.* Washington, D.C.: U.S. Government Printing Office, 1984.
A report concerning child-care needs in the United States and the response to these needs by state, local, and federal governments, as well as the private sector.

Skolnick, A.S., and J.H. Skolnick. *Family in Transition.* Boston: Little, Brown, 1983.
A collection of articles examining changes in the American family, husband-wife relationships, parent-child relationships, lifestyles, and family policy.

Steinfels, M.O. *Who's Minding the Children? The History and Politics of Day Care in America.* New York: Simon & Schuster, 1973.
Extensively researched and documented study of the history of child-care programs in the United States and child-care policy.

Section 2: Two-Career Families

Bernard, J. "The Family: Does It Have a Future, and If So, How Will It Change?" *Radcliffe Quarterly,* Vol. 65, No. 2, (June 1979), pp. 3–6.
The chances are better than ever that the college-educated woman will have a dual-career marriage; she will nonetheless contribute more than her husband does to running the household. If a choice is necessary, his career will take precedence over hers.

Bird, C. *The Two-Paycheck Marriage.* Riverside, N.J.: Rawson, Wade, 1979.

Examines how the two-earner family pattern is changing society and encourages those who are involved in the "most important social revolution of our times."

Hall, F.S., and D.T. Hall. *The Two-Career Couple.* Reading, Mass.: Addison-Wesley, 1979.
Primarily geared to the couple with few children and many economic options. Takes how-to approach in suggesting ways to manage home management, child care, and work conflicts in dual-career lives.

Rapoport, R., and R.N. Rapoport. *Dual-Career Families Re-Examined: New Integrations of Work and Family.* Scranton, Pa.: Harper Colophon Books, 1976.
This is a revised edition of the authors' 1971 publication, *Dual-Career Families.* Recent studies on dual-career families are reviewed, and policy issues are raised. Emphasis is on the increased stress among working mothers due to negligible increase in male participation in domestic work.

White, M.B. *Sharing and Caring: The Art of Raising Kids in Two-Career Families.* Englewood Cliffs, N.J.: Prentice-Hall, 1982.
Describes methods of developing shared parenting and ways to prevent conflict between career and family obligations. Based on the experiences of 46 men and women who practice shared parenting.

Wolfson, R.M., and V. DeLuca. *Couples with Children.* New York: Dembner Books, 1981.
On the basis of their experience with C.O.P.E. (Coping with the Overall Pregnancy/Parenting Experience), the authors discuss the changes, responsibilities, and difficult periods new parents confront.

Section 3: Changing Roles of Mothers and Fathers

Baruch, G., R. Barnett, and C. Rivers. *Lifeprints: New Patterns of Love and Work for Today's Women.* New York: New American Library, 1983.
A study of today's American women examining the issues related to the changes in their lives. Looks at the role of women and their sources of well-being and mastery.

Bell, D. *Being a Man: The Paradox of Masculinity.* Lexington, Mass.: Lewis Publishing, 1982.
Autobiographical account of the author's struggle to understand the new masculinity in light of his own personal relationships. Includes discussions with over 100 men, with a look at how they received their first lessons in masculinity from fathers and male contemporaries.

Bernard, J. *The Future of Motherhood.* New York: Penguin Books, 1974.
Historically, women had no identity crises because their identity as homemakers was prescribed for them by society (unless they were poor or unmarried). As the composition of the female labor force changed, attention focused on the effects of working on motherhood. Bernard points out that women who work out of financial necessity find it easier to integrate work and home roles. For career women, the task is more difficult.

Clary, M. *Daddy's Home.* New York: Seaview Books, 1982.
A personal, moving account of one father's foray into the realm of "motherhood." Clary shares his feelings and experiences as a full-time father. Written for popular audience.

Etaugh, E. "Effects of Nonmaternal Care on Children." *American Psychologist,* Vol. 35, No. 4 (April 1980), pp. 309–319.
Reviews research on effects of nonmaternal care on preschool

children and examines writings in popular press. Data indicate that high-quality nonmaternal care does not appear to have adverse effects on the young child, and a more favorable attitude toward nonmaternal care and working mothers has arisen.

Greenleaf, B.K., with L.A. Schaffer. *HELP: A Handbook for Working Mothers.* New York: Thomas Y. Crowell, 1978.
An attempt at helping mothers overcome the myth of maternal employment being detrimental to family life. The role of the father in the life of his children is emphasized throughout the book.

Lazarre, J. *The Mother Knot.* New York: McGraw-Hill, 1976.
Deals with the ambivalance of the author as she attempts to resolve the problems of mothering and self-fulfillment.

McFadden, M. *Bachelor Fatherhood.* New York: Ace Books, 1974.
Personal account of the author's experience as a single father, with recommendations and advice to other single fathers.

Murray, A.D. "Maternal Employment Reconsidered: Effects on Infants." *American Journal of Orthopsychiatry,* Vol. 45, No. 5 (October 1975), pp. 773–790.
Presents information relating to the need for stability of the caretaker during the infant's first three years. Concludes that stability and consistency are more important in the life of the infant than whether substitute care was used. Maternal separation does not equal maternal deprivation.

Pleck, E., and J. Pleck, eds. *The American Man.* Englewood Cliffs, N.J.: Prentice-Hall, 1980.
Anthology of essays spanning the years from the colonial period to the present. The selections reflect the forces that have influenced men in this country and show how masculine roles have evolved throughout history.

Pleck, J.H. "The Work-Family Role System." *Social Problems,* Vol. 24, No. 4 (April 1977), pp. 417–427.

Reviews the findings of the linkage between work and family.

Singer, W.G., S. Shechtman, and M. Singer. *Real Men Enjoy Their Kids: How to Spend Quality Time with the Children in Your Life*. Nashville, Tenn.: Abingdon Press, 1983.
Encourages fathers and children to spend quality time together in work and play. Includes practical suggestions for sharing household chores, leisure activities, and special family times.

Section 4: Child-Care Selection Guidelines

Auerbach, S. *Choosing Child Care: A Guide for Parents*. New York: Dutton, 1981.
Identifies and defines child-care options; provides checklists to assess the physical facility, emotional climate, learning climate, and social climate.

Baden, R.K., et al. *School Age Child Care: An Action Manual*. Boston: Auburn House, 1982.
A comprehensive how-to book on starting and operating a school-age child-care program.

Endsley, R.C., and M.R. Bradbard. *Quality Day Care: A Handbook of Choices for Parents and Caregivers*. Old Tappan, N.J.: Spectrum, 1981.
Two specialists in the field of child and family development offer a practical guide to help parents select child care. Includes a section on choosing day care for handicapped children, information on special needs of infants and toddlers, and extensive checklists for day-care selection, broken down by age of child.

Filstrup, J.M., with D.W. Gross. *Monday Through Friday: Day Care Alternatives*. Scranton, Pa.: Teachers College Press, 1982.

Case-study format looks at nine child-care options, including playgroups, babysitting cooperatives, nannies, and househusbands. Compares the perspective of parent-consumers and caregivers, providing insight into the advantages and drawbacks of different child-care arrangements.

Galinsky, E., and W.H. Hookd. *The New Extended Family: Day Care That Works.* Boston: Houghton Mifflin, 1978.
A description of different kinds of high-quality child-care programs located across the United States demonstrates viability of child care as a support for working parents.

Greater Minneapolis Day Care Association. *Sick Child Care: Problems and Opportunities.* St. Paul, Minn.
A look at the need for sick-child care, the problems associated with establishing programs, and how to get one started.

Harris, M. "Picking the Best Day Care." *Money,* Vol. 10, No. 8 (August 1981), pp. 60–75.
Concentrates on center-based child care and presents checklist for evaluating centers.

Long, L., and T. Long. *The Handbook for Latchkey Children and Their Parents: A Complete Guide for Latchkey Kids and Their Working Parents.* New York: Arbor House, 1983.
Examines the prevalence of latchkey children in the United States and suggests programs and activities for before- and after-school care. Helps parents assess whether child is capable of latchkey status or should be under supervision.

McKnight, J., and B. Shelsby. "Checking In: An Alternative for Latchkey Kids." *Children Today,* (May–June 1984), pp. 23–25.
Describes a successful check-in latchkey program in Fairfax County, Virginia that may be replicated in other communities.

Mitchell, G. *The Day Care Book: A Guide for Working Parents to Help Them Find the Best Possible Day Care for Their Children.* New York: Stein & Day, 1979.
Addressed specifically to the working parent and written in lay language, the book guides the parent, step by step, through the process of locating, choosing, evaluating, and placing a child in an appropriate day-care program.

Reynolds, J.K. *How to Choose and Use Child Care.* Nashville, Tenn.: Broadman Press, 1980.
Presents information predominantly in a question-and-answer format. Gives advice on choosing child care, with some emphasis placed on compatibility of caregiver's moral and religious beliefs with parents'.

Sigel-Gorelick, B. *The Working Parents' Guide to Child Care.* Boston: Little, Brown, 1983.
A psychologist's detailed examination of the pros and cons of in-home or live-in care, family day care, and center-based child care. Emphasizes need to evaluate arrangements in terms of appropriateness for parent and child. Includes information on how to find selected type of child care and how to make it work.

Section 5: Working Parents

Mackenzie, A., and K.C. Waldo. *About Time! A Woman's Guide to Time Management.* New York: McGraw-Hill, 1981.
Contains a method for determining your timewasters and how to confront them. Chapter 5 (Planning) and Chapter 8 (Delegation) are especially worthwhile for readers who have an aversion to planning and tend to do everything themselves.

Materka, P.R. *Time In, Time Out, Time Enough: A Time Management Guide For Women.* Englewood Cliffs, N.J.: Prentice-Hall, 1982.
Despite its subtitle, this book contains time management sug-

gestions appropriate for everyone. Chapters 17 through 20 are particularly helpful to parents who feel they are working with less support than may be necessary.

Matison, J., and R. Mack. *The Only Barter Book You'll Ever Need.* New York: Bantam Books, 1984.
A good overview of how to barter and set up co-ops and networks.

Olds, S.W. *The Working Parents Survival Guide.* New York: Bantam Books, 1983.
A comprehensive guide that addresses such issues as child-care selection, balancing work and family, the importance of role definitions and planning in marriage, stress and guilt management, and how to enhance organizational and home management skills.

Price, J. *How to Have a Child and Keep Your Job: A Candid Guide for Working Parents.* New York: Penguin Books, 1979.
A reference guide that balances a review of research with practical information for working parents. The initial portion of the book discusses some of the choices working parents confront about roles and responsibilities; the remainder outlines various child-care options and the ways in which society, government, and employers can support working parents.

Princeton Center for Infancy. *Parents' Yellow Pages.* Garden City, N.Y.: Doubleday Anchor, 1979.
Contains useful lists of resources and services for parents. Almost every issue from A to Z that may have an impact on parents is addressed in this helpful guide.

Section 6: Changing Work Environments

Baldwin, D. "The Part-Time Solution." *The Washington Monthly,*
Vol. 16, No. 12, (December 1984), pp. 25–29.
A discussion of the benefits and disadvantages of working part
time after the birth of a child.

Bernstein, P. "The Stress of Relocation: Some Firms Aid
Spouses." *The New York Times,* October 12, 1980.
Talks about companies in Connecticut that are helping relo-
cated spouses find suitable employment in new geographic
areas. Wives are often unwilling or unable to relocate because
their jobs are just as demanding as men's, and pay scales are
not as low as they used to be.

Best, F. "Preferences on Worklife Scheduling and Work-Leisure
Tradeoffs." *Monthly Labor Review,* Vol. 101, No. 6 (June 1978),
pp. 31–37.
A study of 791 county employees in California (doing both
manual and nonmanual work) suggests that workers desire
major changes in the amount and scheduling of time spent on
work, and increased flexibility in scheduling work and non-
work activities over their lifetimes.

Bureau of National Affairs, Inc. *Employers and Child Care: Development of a New Employee Benefit.* Washington, D.C., 1984.
An 80-page report that looks at efforts to provide child-care
assistance as an employee benefit. Profiles experience of employers in developing child-care programs, ranging from on-
site child-care centers to family-oriented personnel policies.
Contains appendix with appropriate IRS rulings, state tax
laws, union bargaining proposals, employer policies, list of
child-care resources, and bibliography.

Cardwell, J.W. "The Other Side of Relocation—Relocating the
Spouse." *Personnel Administrator,* Vol. 25, No. 9 (September
1980), pp. 53–56.

Companies can take several steps to make relocation easier for both the employee and the spouse, including screening, counseling, assisting with reemployment of a working spouse, and financial assistance to ease transition into a new community.

Catalyst Career and Family Center, "Parental Leaves for Child Care" and "Paternity Leaves: A Growing Option." *Catalyst Career and Family Bulletin,* No. 2 (May 1981).
Brief overview of articles on parental and paternity leave, including results of Catalyst's survey of 374 companies. Includes detailed information on several firms offering paternity leave to fathers.

Cohen, A., and H. Gadon. *Alternative Work Schedules: Integrating Individual and Organization Needs.* Reading, Mass.: Addison-Wesley, 1978.
Discusses the advantages and disadvantages of flexible and staggered working hours, the compressed week, permanent part-time work, and job sharing; describes how to select work schedules that meet the needs of the organization and the preferences of employees.

Friedman, D. "The Child-Care Challenge: How Are We Really Doing?" *Working Woman,* Vol. 9, No. 9 (November 1984), pp. 210–215.
An update on recent changes in child care: consumer attitudes, employer attitudes, the role of government, the pressing needs for specific types of child care, and how those needs are being met.

_____ . *Encouraging Employer Supports to Working Parents: Community Strategies for Change.* New York: Center for Public Advocacy Research, 1983.
Analysis of innovative programs and approaches by employers to the issues of employed parents in five cities.

Gallese, L.R. "Employees Get Help on Delicate Balance of Work and Family." *The Wall Street Journal,* April 3, 1980.
Talks about working-parent seminars being sponsored by Wheelock College to help parent-employees balance work and family.

"Guess Who Can Get Off When the Baby's Coming?" *Insurance Worker,* Vol. 21 (April 5, 1979).
Prudential's leave-of-absence policy not only covers female employees during pregnancy but also grants fathers paternity leave before, during, or after the baby arrives, but not for more than six months.

Kamerman, S.B., A.J. Kahn, and P. Kingston. *Maternity Policies and Working Women.* New York: Columbia University Press, 1983.
Detailed analysis of maternity policies in the United States as compared to other countries. Presents the history of maternity policies, employer and employee perspectives in the private sector, and current state and federal provisions; also reports results of a survey of a nationwide sample of 250 companies. Includes brief notes on paternity leave. A reference source for maternity and paternity-leave policies.

Leeds, M.H. "Child Care Leaves." *Personnel Administrator,* Vol. 29, No. 5 (May 1984), pp. 5–8.
Describes the range of child-care leaves developed to meet current social, economic, and legal realities: pregnancy disability leave, maternity leave, baby bonus, and flexible timing of child-care leaves.

LeRoux, M. "Day Care Center Nurtures Savings, Worker Goodwill." *Business Insurance,* Vol. 14, No. 3, (December 15, 1980), p. 3.
A child-care center for employees' children has brought many benefits to PCA International in Charlotte, N.C., including

$30,000 a year in reduced employee turnover, a competitive recruitment advantage, and improved employee morale. Financial and program statistics are cited.

Lund, S. "Kids and Careers." *Working Woman,* July 1982, pp. 54–57.
Describes the experiences of four parents who chose to work part time: the problems encountered in doing so, the advantages, and the response of employers.

Magid, R.Y. *Child Care Initiatives for Working Parents: Why Employers Get Involved.* An American Management Association Survey Report. New York: AMACOM, 1983.
A study of employers in the United States who got involved in a variety of child-care initiatives for working parents. Examines the reasons why employers got involved in the issue of work and family and the benefits reported by employers as a result.

_____ . *Parents and Employers: New Partners in Child Care.* New York: AMACOM, 1982.
Describes the experiences of a group of employers who formed a consortium in order to implement a worksite child-care center. Also looks at the steps to follow in starting a worksite child-care project.

Margolis, D.R. *The Managers: Corporate Life in America.* New York: Morrow, 1979.
A sociologist examines the tyranny of the corporation over the life of the executive, and its equally threatening concomitant, the tyranny of the executive's life over that of his family. Describes how the structure of a typical corporate career cuts a manger off from competing social structures, including those of his family and his community.

McCroskey, J. "Work and Families: What Is the Employer's Responsibility?" *Personnel Journal,* Vol. 61, No. 1 (January 1982), pp. 30–38.

Explores the ways in which an employer can help employees balance work and family responsibilities: what's possible, and how to develop and implement a child-care assistance program.

McIntyre, K.J. "Day Care: An Employer Benefit, Too." *Business Insurance,* Vol. 12, No. 3 (December 11, 1978), p. 11.
In addition to offering employers better employee attendance and punctuality and a more stable workforce, employment-related day care offers working parents peace of mind.

Nollen, S.I. *New Work Schedules in Practice.* New York: Van Nostrand Reinhold, 1982.
Overview of issues dealing with alternative work schedules, directed to managerial decision makers.

Norman, N., and J.T. Tedesche. "Paternity Leave: The Unpopular Benefit Option." *Personnel Administrator,* Vol. 29, No. 2 (February 1984), pp. 39–43.
Reviews the rise in the number of companies offering paternity leave and the reasons why it is still underutilized.

Remesch-Allnutt, K. "Day Care That Works." *American Baby,* Vol. 46, No. 2 (February 1984), pp. 46–68.
Suggestions for the parent-employee who wants to convince his or her employer to establish an on-site child-care center.

Staines, G.L., and J. Pleck, II. *The Impact of Work Schedules on the Family.* Ann Arbor, Mich.: Institute for Social Research, 1983.
Findings from the first systematic study of the effects of work schedules on family stress. Includes examination of the relationship between mother's and father's work schedules and the amount of time they spend taking care of children, doing housework, and fulfilling other family roles.

Vrazo, F. "Sick-Child Care: A Helping Hand to Soothe a Fevered Brow." *The Philadelphia Inquirer* (February 8, 1986)

Appendix C
Selected Resource Organizations

The following is a selected list of organizations and agencies that can provide working parents and employers with one or more services: information, support services, technical assistance, educational services, and training.

Amalgamated Clothing and
  Textile Workers Union
Social Service Department
15 Union Square
New York, NY 10003
(212) 242-0700

American Academy of Child
  Psychiatry
3615 Wisconsin Avenue, N.W.
Washington, DC 20016
(202) 966-7300

American Academy of
  Pediatrics
P.O. Box 1037
Evanston, IL 60009
(312) 869-9327

American College of Nurse/
  Midwives
1522 K Street, N.W.
Washington, DC 20005
(202) 347-5445

Bank Street College of
  Education
Day Care Consultation
  Service
610 W. 112th Street
New York, NY 10025
(212) 663-7200

Beaver College
Department of Education
Classroom Building, Room
  315
Work-Family Partnerships
Intergenerational Programs
  Project
Glenside, PA 19038
(215) 572-2938

Bureau of National Affairs,
  Inc.
1231 25th Street N.W.
Washington, DC 20037
(202) 452-4985

Catalyst Career and Family
  Center
Corporate Child Care
  Resources
14 E. 60th Street
New York, NY 10022
(212) 759-9700

Center for Pubic Advocacy
  Research
12 W. 37th Street
New York, NY 10018
(212) 564-9220

Childbirth Education
  Association
P.O. Box 1609
Springfield, VA 22151
(703) 941-7183

Childcare Action Campaign
P.O. Box 313
New York, NY 10185
(212) 354-1225

Child Care Law Center
625 Market Street, Suite 816
San Francisco, CA 94105
(415) 495-5498

Child Care Resource Center
24 Thorndike Street
Cambridge, MA 20141
(617) 547-1057

Child Care Resource and
  Referral Network
320 Judah Street, Suite 2
San Francisco, CA 94122
(415) 566-1226

Child Nutrition Division
U.S. Department of
  Agriculture
Washington, DC 20250
(202) 655-4000

Children's Bureau
U.S. Department of Labor
Washington, DC 20210
(202) 523-6666

Children's Defense Fund
122 C Street, N.W.
Washington, DC 20001
(202) 483-1470

Child Welfare League of
America
67 Irving Place
New York, NY 10003
(212) 254-7410

Coalition of Labor Union
Women
15 Union Square
New York, NY 10003
(212) 242-0700

Council for Exceptional
Children (CEC)
1920 Association Drive
Reston, VA 20091
(703) 620-3660

Family Matters Project
Department of Human
Development and Family
Studies
Cornell University
Ithaca, NY 14853
(607) 256-7610

Family Resource Coalition
230 N. Michigan Avenue,
Suite 1625
Chicago, IL 60601
(312) 726-4750

National Association for the
Education of Young
Children
1834 Connecticut Avenue,
N.W.
Washington, DC 20009
(202) 232-8777

National Association for
Family Day Care
41 Dunbar Street
Manchester, NH 03103
(603) 622-4408

National Association of
Hospital Affiliated Child
Care Programs
204 N. Forest Street
Batavia, IL 60510
(312) 879-6158

National Black Child
Development Institute
1463 Rhode Island Avenue,
N.W.
Washington, DC 20005
(202) 387-1281

National Coalition for
Campus Childcare
UWM Day Care Center,
Room 200
University of Wisconsin at
Milwaukee,
P.O. Box 413
Milwaukee, WI 53201
(414) 963-5384

National Committee for Prevention of Child Abuse
332 S. Michigan Avenue, Suite 1250
Chicago, IL 60604
(312) 663-3520

National Federation of Business and Professional Women's Clubs
2012 Massachusetts Avenue, N.W.
Washington, DC 20036
(202) 293-1100

National Organization for Women
Task Force on Child Care
45 Newbury Street
Boston, MA 02116
(617) 965-1713

New Ways to Work
149 Ninth Street
San Francisco, CA 94103
(415) 552-1000

Parents in the Workplace
906 N. Dale Street
St. Paul, MN 55103
(612) 488-7284

San Antonio Coalition for Children, Youth and Families
1101 W. Woodlawn Street, Room 205
San Antonio, TX 78219
(512) 732-1051

Save The Children/The Child Care Support Center
11826 W. Peachtree Street, N.W.
Suite 209
Atlanta, GA 30309
(404) 885-1578

Sick Child Care Project
MMC and Associates
1800 Red Maple Grove
Ambler, PA 19002
(215) 643-5272

School Age Child Care Project
Center for Research on Women
Wellesley College
828 Washington Street
Wellesley, MA 02180
(617) 431-1453

Texas Institute for Families, Inc.
111311 Richmond, L-107
Houston, TX 77082
(713) 497-8719

Well Baby Clinics
(Check your phone book under "Government," City or State:
"Maternal-Child Health")

Women's Bureau
U.S. Department of Labor
Office of the Secretary
Washington, DC 02010
(202) 523-8916

Work/Family Directions
Child Care Referral Service
200 The Riverway
Boston, MA 02215
(617) 734-0001

Work and Family
  Information Center
The Conference Board
845 Third Avenue
New York, NY 10022
(212) 759-0900

Appendix D
Research Centers for Work/Family Issues and Child Development

Bank Street College of
   Education
Work and Family Life Study
610 W. 112th Street
New York, NY 10025
(212) 663-7202

Beaver College
Employer Initiatives for
   Child Care Project
Department of Education
Glenside, PA 19038
(215) 572-2938

Brown University
Child Behavior Research
   Lab
Providence, RI 02912
(401) 421-8241

Center for Public Advocacy
   Research, Inc.
Working Parents Project
12 W. 37th Street
New York, NY 10018
(212) 564-9220

Columbia University
School of Social Work
Cross National Studies
  Project (212) 280-5449
Industrial Social Welfare
  Center (212) 280-5173
622 W. 113th Street
New York, NY 10025

The Conference Board
Work and Family
  Information Center
845 Third Avenue
New York, NY 10022
(212) 759-0900

Demonstration and Research
  Center for Early
  Childhood Education
George Peabody College for
  Teachers
P.O. Box 151
Nashville, TN 37203
(615) 322-8125

Employee Benefit Research
  Institute
2121 K Street, N.W.
Washington, DC 20036
(202) 659-0670

Fels Research Institute for
  the Study of Human
  Development
1005 Xenia Avenue
Yellow Springs, OH 45387
(513) 767-7324

Frank Porter Graham Child
  Development Center
University of North Carolina
Chapel Hill, NC 27514
(919) 942-3279

Howard University
Child Development Center
310 Prospect Street
New Haven, CT 06510
(203) 777-3481

Howard University
Child Development Center
2217 Fourth Street, N.W.
Washington, DC 20001
(202) 636-7565

Kansas Center for Research
  in Early Childhood
  Education
University of Kansas
Lawrence, KS 66045
(913) 864-4295

John F. Kennedy Child
  Development Center
4200 E. Ninth Avenue
University of Colorado
Denver, CO 80220
(303) 556-2800

Merrill-Palmer Institute
St. John's Hall, Suite 200
Catholic University of
  America
Washington, DC 20064
(202) 635-5453

National Institute of Child
  Health and Human
  Development
U.S. Department of HEW
9000 Rockville Park
Bethesda, MD 20014
(301) 496-4000

University of Arkansas
Center for Early
  Development and
  Education
College of Education
815 Sherman Street
Little Rock, AR 72202
(501) 569-3000

University of Maryland
Institute of Child Study
College Park, MD 20742
(301) 454-2034

University of Washington
Child Development and
  Mental Retardation
  Center
Seattle, WA 98195
(206) 543-2100

Wellesley College
Center for Research on
  Women
Wellesley, MA 02181
(617) 235-0320

Wheelock College Center for
  Parenting Studies
200 The Riverway
Boston, MA 02215
(617) 734-5200

Yale University
Child Study Center
333 Cedar Street
New Haven, CT 06510
(203) 785-2513

Appendix E

Current State Licensing Offices for Child-Care Centers

By writing to the office in your state, you can obtain a complete list of all licensed child-care centers in your area.

ALABAMA

Office of Program
    Administration
64 North Union Street
Montgomery, AL 36130
(205) 832-6150

ALASKA

Department of Health and
    Social Services

Pouch H-05
Juneau, AK 99811
(907) 465-3206

ARIZONA

Arizona Department of
    Health Services
1740 West Adams
Phoenix, AZ 85007
(602) 255-1112

ARKANSAS

Department of Social and
  Rehabilitative Services
P.O. Box 1487
Little Rock, AR 72203
(501) 371-7512

CALIFORNIA

Department of Social
  Services
744 P Street
Mail Station 17-17
Sacramento, CA 95814
(916) 322-8538

COLORADO

Department of Social
  Services
1575 Sherman Street, Room
  420
Denver, CO 80203
(303) 839-3361

CONNECTICUT

State Department of Health
79 Elm Street
Hartford, CT 06115
(203) 566-2535

DELAWARE

Department of Health and
  Social Services
P.O. Box 309
Wilmington, DE 19899
(302) 421-6786

DISTRICT OF COLUMBIA

Licensing and Certification
  Division
Social Services Branch
1406 L Street, N.W., 2nd
  Floor
Washington, DC 20005
(202) 727-0672

FLORIDA

Department of Health and
  Rehabilitation Services
1311 Winewood Boulevard
Tallahassee, FL 32301
(904) 488-1850

GEORGIA

Department of Human
  Resources
618 Ponce de Leon Avenue
Atlanta, GA 30308
(404) 894-5144

GUAM

Division of Social Services
P.O. Box 2816
Agana, GU 96910
(671) 734-9912

HAWAII

Department of Social
  Services and Housing
P.O. Box 339
Honolulu, HI 96809
(808) 548-2302

IDAHO

Department of Health and
   Welfare
Statehouse
Boise, ID 83720
(208) 334-4076

ILLINOIS

Department of Children and
   Family Services
1 North Old State Capitol
   Plaza
Springfield, IL 62706
(217) 785-2598

INDIANA

State Department of Public
   Welfare
100 North Senate Avenue,
   Room 701
Indianapolis, IN 46204
(317) 232-4421

IOWA

Department of Social
   Services
3619½ Douglass Avenue
Des Moines, IA 50310
(515) 281-5581

KANSAS

Division of Health and
   Environment
Building 740, Forbes AFB
Topeka, KS 66620
(913) 862-9360

KENTUCKY

Department of Human
   Resources
Fourth Floor East
275 East Main Street
Frankfort, KY 40601
(502) 564-2800

LOUISIANA

Department of Health and
   Human Resources
P.O. Box 3767
Baton Rouge, LA 70821
(504) 342-6446

MAINE

Department of Human
   Services
Augusta, ME 04333
(207) 289-3455

MARYLAND

Department of Health and
   Mental Hygiene
201 West Preston Street
Baltimore, MD 21201
(301) 383-4009

MASSACHUSETTS

Office for Children
120 Boylston Street
Boston, MA 02116
(617) 727-8956

MICHIGAN

Michigan Department of
  Social Services
116 West Allegan
P.O. Box 80037
Lansing, MI 48926
(517) 373-8300

MINNESOTA

Department of Public
  Welfare
Centennial Office Building,
  4th Floor
St. Paul, MN 55155
(612) 296-2539

MISSISSIPPI

State Board of Health
P.O. Box 1700
Jackson, MS 39205
(601) 982-6505

MISSOURI

State Department of Social
  Services
Broadway State Office
  Building
303 W. McCarthy Street
Jefferson City, MO 65103
(314) 751-2450

MONTANA

Montana Department of
  Social and Rehabilitation
  Services
P.O. Box 4210
Helena, MT 59601
(406) 449-3865

NEBRASKA

Department of Public
  Welfare
P.O. Box 95026
Lincoln, NB 68509
(402) 471-3121

NEVADA

Division of Youth Services
505 E. King Street
Carson City, NV 89710
(702) 885-5911

NEW HAMPSHIRE

Office of Social Services
Hazen Drive
Concord, NH 03301
(603) 271-4402

NEW JERSEY

New Jersey Department of
  Human Services
1 South Montgomery Street
Trenton, NJ 08623
(609) 292-1879

NEW MEXICO

Health and Environmental
  Department
440 Chamisa Hill Building
Suite S-3
Santa Fe, NM 87504
(505) 827-3431

NEW YORK

New York State Department
  of Social Services
40 North Pearl Street
Albany, NY 12243
(800) 342-3715

NORTH CAROLINA

Office of Child Day Care
  Licensing
1919 Ridge Road
Raleigh, NC 27607
(919) 733-4801

NORTH DAKOTA

Children and Family
  Services
Russell Building—Box 7
Highway 83 North
Bismarck, ND 58505
(701) 224-3580

OHIO

Bureau of Licensing and
  Standards
30 E. Broad Street, 30th
  Floor
Columbus, OH 43215
(614) 466-3822

OKLAHOMA

Department of Public
  Welfare
P.O. Box 25352
Oklahoma City, OK 73125
(405) 521-3561

OREGON

Department of Human
  Resources
198 Commercial Street, S.E.
Salem, OR 97310
(503) 378-3178

PENNSYLVANIA

Pennsylvania Department of
  Public Welfare
Room 423, Health and
  Welfare Building
Harrisburg, PA 17120
(717) 961-4371

PUERTO RICO

P.O. Box 11398
Fernandez Juncos Station
Santurce, PR 00910
(809) 723-2127

RHODE ISLAND

Department of Social and
  Rehabilitative Services
610 Mount Pleasant Avenue
Providence, RI 02908
(401) 277-3446

SOUTH CAROLINA

South Carolina Department
of Social Services
P.O. Box 1520
Columbia, SC 29202
(803) 758-7620

SOUTH DAKOTA

Department of Social
Services
Richard F. Kneip Building
Pierre, SD 57501
(605) 773-3227

TENNESSEE

Tennessee Department of
Human Services
111-19 7th Avenue North
Nashville, TN 37203
(615) 741-3284

TEXAS

Texas Department of
Human Resources
P.O. Box 2960
Austin, TX 78769
(512) 441-3355

UTAH

Division of Family Services
P.O. Box 2500
Salt Lake City, UT 84110
(801) 533-5031

VERMONT

Department of Social and
Rehabilitative Services
81 River Street
Montpelier, VT 05602
(802) 241-2158

VIRGINIA

Department of Welfare
8007 Discovery Drive
Richmond, VA 23229
(804) 281-9025

VIRGIN ISLANDS

Department of Social
Services
P.O. Box 530
Charlotte Amalie
St. Thomas, VI 00801
(809) 774-0930

WASHINGTON

The Department of Social
and Health Services
State Office Building #2
Mail Stop 440
Olympia, WA 98504
(106) 753-7160

WEST VIRGINIA

Department of Welfare
1900 Washington Street, E.
Charlestown, WV 25305
(304) 348-7980

WISCONSIN

Division of Community
  Services
1 West Wilson Street
Madison, WI 53702
(608) 266-8200

WYOMING

Division of Public Assistance
  and Social Services
Hathway Building
Cheyenne, WY 82002
(307) 777-7561

Appendix F
Selected Periodicals List

*Catalyst Career and Family
    Bulletin*
Catalyst
14 E. 60th Street
New York, NY 10022

Child Care Information Exchange
P.O. Box 2890
Redmond, WA 98073

*Child Care Information &
    Referral Issues*
320 Judah Street, Suite 2
San Francisco, CA 94122

Childhood Education
Association for Childhood
    Education International
3615 Wisconsin Avenue., N.W.
Washington, DC 20016

Children Today
Office of Human Services
U.S. Department of Health
    and Human Services
200 Independence Avenue
    Room 356G
Washington, DC 20001

*Children's Defense
    Fund Reports*
122 C Street, N.W.
Washington, DC 20001

Day Care and Early Education
Human Science Press
72 Fifth Avenue
New York, NY 10010

Day Care USA Resources Newsletter
Day Care Information Service
8701 Georgia Avenue
Suite 800
Silver Spring, MD 20910

Family Resource Bulletin
Family Resource Coalition
230 N. Michigan Avenue
Suite 1625
Chicago, IL 60601

Nexus
Parent in the Workplace
1006 West Lake
Minneapolis, MN 55408

Report on Preschool Programs
The Biweekly Newsletter of Programs for Early Childhood Development
1300 N. 17th Street
Arlington, VA 22209

Business Link: Report on Management
Initiatives for Working Parents
Resources for Child Care Management
P.O. Box 669
Summit, NJ 07901

World of Work Report
Work in America Institute, Inc.
700 White Plains Road
Scarsdale, NY 10583

Young Children
National Association for the Education of Young Children
1834 Connecticut Avenue, N.W.
Washington, DC 20009

Free Pamphlets

A chart listing a dozen of the most common diseases and their symptoms, treatment, and prevention appears in the free pamphlet *Memo to Parents About Immunization*. Write to:

Metropolitan Life Insurance Company
Health and Welfare Division
1 Madison Avenue
New York, NY 10010

Another free booklet: *Childhood Diseases.* Write to:

Prudential Insurance Company
5 Prudential Place
Newark, NJ 07101

Notes

1. *Current Population Reports: Household and Family Characteristics,* Series P-20, No. 398 (Washington, D.C.: U.S. Department of Commerce, Bureau of Census, March 1984).
2. U. Bronfenbrenner, "On Making Human Beings Human," from *Character II* (Illinois: Fulco-Midwest, 1980), pp. 1-7.
3. E.T. Devine, "The Day Nursery," from *Charities Review,* Volume 10, Number 8 (August 1927), pp. 263-265.
4. D. Fisher, *Mothers and Children* (New York: Holt & Company, 1914), p. 58.
5. O. English et al., *Fathers Are Parents Too* (New York: Belmont Books, 1951), p. 103.
6. A. Van Buren, *Dear Abbey on Marriage* (New York: McGraw-Hill, 1962), p. 47.
7. E. Trueblood and P. Trueblood, *The Recovery of Family Life* (New York: Harper & Row, 1953), p. 26.
8. P. Drucker, "Unmaking the Nineteenth Century," *The Wall Street Journal* (July 6, 1981).
9. D. Bell, *Being a Man: The Paradox of Masculinity* (Lexington, Mass.: Lewis Publishing, 1982), p. 19.
10. United Media Enterprises Report on Leisure in America (New York: Reports and Forecasts, 1983)
11. H.L. Mencken, *In Defense of Women* (New York: Time Inc., 1963) pp. 72-77.
12. D. Friedman, "Corporate Financial Assistance for Child Care"

(New York: Conference Board Work and Family Information Center, 1986), pp. 5–9.

13. B. Robey, *The American People* (New York: Dutton, 1985), p. 10.
14. D. Bell, op. cit., p. 61.
15. M. Maccoby, *The Gamesman* (New York: Simon & Schuster, 1976).
16. W. Whyte, *The Organization Man* (New York: Simon & Schuster, 1956), p. 23.
17. G. Baruch, R. Barnett, and C. Rivers, *Lifeprints: New Patterns of Love and Work for Today's Women* (New York: New American Library, 1983), pp. 133–136.
18. S. LaFollette, *Concerning Women* (New York: A. and C. Bone Co., 1926), p. 211.
19. C. Clark, *Idea Management: How to Motivate Creativity and Motivation* (New York: AMACOM, 1980).
20. W. Phillips, *The American Scene: A Reader* (New York: Vintage Press, 1982), pp. 347–349.
21. L.B. Bohlke, ed., *Willa Cather In Person: Interviews, Speeches, and Letters* (Nebraska: University of Nebraska Press, 1986).
22. J. Naisbitt and P. Aburdene, *Reinventing the Corporation* (New York: Waiver Books, 1985), pp. 36–46; 297–299.
23. D. Weil, "Real Life Supercouples," from *Working Mother* (July 1985), pp. 60–63.

Index

195